CHAMELEON

The Boy George Story

CHAMELEON

The Boy George Story

by
SALLY
BROMPTON

Spellmount

In the same illustrated series
WEATHER REPORT
DOLLY PARTON
ELLA FITZGERALD

© Sally Brompton 1984

First published in the UK by
SPELLMOUNT LTD
12 Dene Way, Speldhurst,
Tunbridge Wells, Kent TN3 0NX

ISBN 0-946771-91-X PB
Designed and produced by
Susan Ryall

British Library Cataloguing in Publication Data

Brompton, Sally
    Chameleon: the story of Boy George.
    1. Boy George   2. Rock musicians –
    England – Biography
    I. Title
    784.5'0092'4   ML420.B757

    ISBN 0-946771-91-X

Contents

Acknowledgements

Very many thanks to all the people without whose reminiscences – both personal and panoramic – this book could never have been conceived. Also for the access to their photo albums. In particular: The Arnolds, especially Jane, Terry, Lennie, Beryl, Andrea, Susan and Mandy; The Ealing Contingent, especially Nicola, Selena and Dij; Peter Dawson, Su Cankett, Marianne Atterton, Mick Strevens, Sharon Walker and David Brenchley for their memories of George's schooldays; Tracy Burch, Troy Morris, Michael Eggleton, Andy Polaris, Kirk Brandon, Steve Strange, Melissa Caplan, Stephen Jones, Stewart Mechem, Peter Small, Lizzie Joyce, Sue Clowes, Ashley Goodall, Ann Bishop, Len Fletcher and, of course, the indefatigable A-Team. And all the other people who gave me so much invaluable information both on and off the record. Thanks also to my colleagues in Fleet Street and elsewhere who helped to fill in the gaps, and to Philip Sallon, his family, Michael Parkinson and Channel 10 Television for an unforgettable evening in Dollis Hill.

Prologue

When Boy George arrived in the United States he was compared to The Beatles. When he reached Australia it was more like the Second Coming. In a land where the prototype male is a cross between Rocky Marciano and Brendan Behan, this made-up, self-acclaimed "poofter with muscles" was mobbed, mauled and all but massacred by adoring fans of both sexes. From Tokyo to Torquay Boy George is worshipped, imitated and, most important of all, talked about constantly. In less time than it takes most pop groups to produce a first record he has achieved the kind of celebrity normally reserved for heroes, angels and visiting royalty. Yet he appears to be a travesty of all that is commonly considered to be either wholesome or commercial. In his own words "if there is such a thing as a weirdo, I suppose I'm one in every way". And his widespread popularity, breaking through all accepted barriers of taste and understanding, has astounded the music industry and sociologists alike.

Certainly, the extraordinary success of Boy George cannot be measured in musical terms alone. While still in his professional infancy, George has become an international media requisite, a show-business legend and an everyday, frequently controversial, ingredient of public life.

Musically, Boy George and his band, Culture Club, break records as fast as they make them. Their first hit, *Do You Really Want To Hurt Me?* topped the charts in fifty-one of the fifty-two countries where it was released. Their next big success, *Karma*

Before the Boy. George O'Dowd as he appeared in Vogue in 1980

Chameleon, sold a million copies in three weeks in Britain alone, selling more records faster, than anyone else had done for over a decade. At the age of twenty-two, George became a millionaire quicker than any other star including The Beatles and Elvis Presley.

Yet, it is the man himself who fascinates and intrigues the world. The real Boy George is a mystery to all but his family and a tiny circle of close friends. His monstrous success has caused him to pull a veil of ambiguity over his life as well as his appearance in ironic contrast to his natural instinct to be entirely frank about everything – especially himself.

His private life, too, is full of contrasts, encompassing both his similarity individual-astic friends and his down-to-earth working-class family. He relies heavily on both to help him to maintain his level-headed approach to his success. When the two worlds meet – as he has always intended they should – the results are frequently bizarre. Such an occasion was the first time his parents, Jerry and Dina O'Dowd, met his best friend, Philip Sallon.

George took Philip, a master of outrageous eccentricity, back to his family's end-of-terrace house in suburban Shooters Hill. Clad in a long flowing cloak and tricorne hat Philip swept into the narrow cluttered hallway in the manner of a visiting potentate. Without a word he plonked himself down at the O'Dowds' untuned piano, lifting his hands high above his head ready to bring them crashing down, maestro-style, on to his keys, when George's father, a builder by trade, stuck his head round the door. "Tea or coffee?" enquired Jerry impassively.

Philip's hands froze over the keys. "Aren't you shocked?" he demanded, puzzled.

Jerry shrugged. "I've seen many many nutcases in my time. What do you want, tea or coffee, boy?"

The incident illustrates the disparity between George's perfectly ordinary background and his extraordinary friends. Yet, thanks to his own strong character and integrity, he has blended the two worlds into one, forming an almost impenetrable security blanket to help him to withstand the pressures of fame. And it is this solid backdrop that has provided Boy George with the strength and stability to become the international star he is today. His influence is enormous – both on his admirers and those around him – to such an extent that he can dominate an entire evening's proceedings without even being present . . .

12 July, 1984

Philip Sallon was having one of those days.

His sister Sarah had just arrived home unexpectedly from Israel, Michael Parkinson was trying to do a television interview of his family in the back room, there was a recording contract in the offing, and now George had lost Marilyn.

While an anxious all-macho Australian television man tried vainly to get him to lower his voice, Philip was gabbling down the pay telephone in the hall, trying to placate George and relay a string of messages at the same time.

"I've told you, George, Marilyn's trying to get in touch with you. Why don't we meet for a meal somewhere . . . And Virginia wants to know what's happening for your birthday." The words tumbled over one another like a verbal roller-coaster while the television man flapped his arms despairingly in Philip's direction.

In the living room, Mrs Sallon, grey-haired and gaunt-faced, was telling Michael Parkinson and several million Australians exactly what she thought about George.

"I like Boy George because he's the same now as he was seven years ago. He's become successful but he's just the same George as he always was and I respect that. I like him a lot. We all love him. . ."

The television crew had transformed the lounge of the North London semi into a makeshift studio. Wires snaked across the red and gold patterned carpet and three powerful spotlights bounced off a huge silver umbrella lighting up the chintzy clutter and the artificial flowers.

"Which frock shall I wear tonight?" George with best friend, Philip Sallon

Just off-camera a tea-tray was laid out with cream cakes and the best china. In this household Michael Parkinson was a bigger celebrity than Boy George.

Philip tiptoed back into the room in time to hear his mother singing George's praises.

"Boy George came here on Sunday and left all the newspapers after he had looked through them for photographs of himself. He's a good boy to his parents and he doesn't crow. . . They all sing, you know. . ." she added irrelevantly, thrusting a hand in the direction of Philip and his sisters, ". . .and my husband's in the synagogue choir."

An evening in Dollis Hill starring Michael Parkinson and the Sallon family

Without a warning the whole family broke lustily into a rousing Jewish folk song. Michael Parkinson listened politely, a smile frozen on his lips, while the half-dozen technicians gazed at each other despondently. Boy George, Marilyn and several of the current batch of London night-clubs were in the bag – including Philip's own Mud Club. All they needed now was Philip and his family to complete their documentary – which they had temporarily entitled *Gender Bender* but tactfully rechristened *The London Scene*.

"I think we've come up against a challenge that's bigger than we are," murmured the director grimly.

"I'm forever blowing bubbles," sang Philip, "pretty little bubbles in the air. . ."

"Mrs Sallon, I'm asking you about Boy George," continued Parkinson, resolutely ignoring the musical interlude.

"I like him because he hasn't lost his head with his success," said Philip's mother. "If ever there've been problems with Philip – and there have been plenty of problems with Philip – I can always talk to Boy George and he's always been very helpful and understanding."

Tonight Philip was dressed casually in baggy cheesecloth trousers with holes in the back and a loose black top covered with weird squiggles. His long black hair fluffed around his face, pale without make-up.

"I don't like Philip's green hair and I don't like the crazy clothes," his mother was telling Parkinson. "He's a wonderful wonderful portrait artist. He's as good as my husband is a caricaturist. And he is also a very, very talented actor and with those two qualities I think he could do better than going around looking like a lunatic."

"Have you had trouble with the neighbours and that sort of thing?" asked Parkinson.

"Well, everyone always goes very quiet when it comes to Philip and then, when the subject is approached – by me – they say 'Oh, well, Mrs Sallon, in this day and age . . . what can you do with them?' I only hope he turns out all right in the end."

Philip, Marilyn and George are best friends. Not lovers but the kind of best friends you have at school – sharing secrets, giggling, gossiping, bitching, back-biting, swapping clothes and make-up ideas.

Philip, the nice Jewish boy from Dollis Hill, extrovert innovator of the London nightclub scene, leader of outrageous fashion, professional purveyor of fun, fun, fun;

Marilyn, the sultry blonde singer who made his name dressing like M. Monroe and kept it because "a boy named Marilyn is controversial, isn't it?";

And George. The working-class lad from south-east London who dressed outrageously and became a celebrity. And then a singer. And then a superstar. And then a sensation. Boy George a phenomenon of our time.

The television crew had moved upstairs to Philip's bedroom, a tiny wardrobe of a room with all the paraphernalia of narcissism. Philip was back on the telephone in the hall, cramming ten-pence pieces into the slot, frantically ringing round London in search of Marilyn. Michael Parkinson was drinking tea at the kitchen table and being interviewed by Mrs Sallon. Sarah was defending her brother to anyone who cared to listen.

"He's always had a popular personality," said Sarah. "He's extremely talented so he attracts people to him like a magnet. He can't help it. He's always had this magnetic draw for people. He amuses them. He makes us laugh. Philip could make a corpse laugh."

Upstairs the camera crew were near to tears.

Philip's bedroom was unprepared for its debut before the great Australian public. There were cosmetics everywhere, spilling out of tin boxes, piled on shelves and crammed in drawers. A tube of hair gel glitter had fallen on the floor. Copies of *Vogue* lay scattered among a heap of fashion books, a red-sequined skull cap dangled over the dressing-table mirror while a wild variety of outlandish outfits were squashed together on the clothes rail.

Prised away from the telephone at last

Philip sat on his cluttered bed rooting through plastic bags stuffed with photographs and newspaper cuttings about himself.

"Was that what you were wearing last week?" enquired the director gazing impassively at Philip's get-up.

"Yes, this is the outfit," said Philip critically studying a photograph of himself wearing a tinsel crown.

"All right. Then we'll do the clothes' sequence. It's an excuse to show off the clothes. We can have you flicking through the rack going 'adidadidadida'. . ."

"Which frock shall I wear tonight?" minced Philip sarcastically.

"Exactly."

"Oh – it's all so plastic, isn't it. I'm sorry. . ."

"You're so cynical."

"It is, though, isn't it? Like Beau Brummell going through his clothes. It's pathetic. I'm sorry – I'm not being awful."

Downstairs, Sarah, a doctor by day and a singer in a Jerusalem jazz club by night, pounded the piano.

"Could you tell her to stop playing the piano!" shouted David.

"It sounds like home, though, doesn't it?" said Philip helpfully. "If you hear noises in the background it sounds like home."

"It's hard for editing," said the director, keeping his temper.

"Kill the piano!" yelled someone down the stairs.

"This is unreal, isn't it," giggled Philip.

"Right," said the director. "Everyone ready?"

The lights came on, the clapper-board snapped shut, the cameras whirred, the telephone rang.

"Damn," said the director as Philip shot out of the door.

"It's George," screamed Mrs Sallon up the stairs.

This time Sarah beat her brother to the phone.

"A boy named Marilyn . . ."

"George. Hello, darling. I'm back from Israel. Listen, my boss says if you come to Israel in August, he's going to throw a huge party. Try, try. He's got a fantastic house, too."

In the kitchen Mrs Sallon was still talking about George. "I've known Boy George seven years and he comes here plenty. He's here practically every other night of the week. I'll come in sometimes and he'll be sitting here and I start screaming and he says 'all right, all right – we'll do the dishes'. I never kow-tow to him. When I let rip I let rip at the whole lot of them."

Michael Parkinson had escaped back to his Berkshire mansion. The television crew passed around cigarettes and listened wearily to Philip giving George a detailed rundown on his efforts to trace the elusive Marilyn. When he hung up he was full of apologies.

Back in his bedroom he sat down obediently at his dressing table and began ripping up copies of the *Daily Mirror*, tying his hair up in the strips while one of the television men sneaked downstairs and took the telephone receiver off the hook.

"When did you first notice Philip's flamboyance?" Michael Parkinson had earlier asked Ralph Sallon, a well-known caricaturist for the very newspaper his son was now weaving into his coiffure.

"When he refused to go through with anything that is normal," replied white-haired Mr Sallon. "When I first realised that he had not quite the normal brain. . ."

The television team managed to capture several seconds of Philip making-up on film before he disappeared to make his next call.

"George was looking for him so I said I'd try a few numbers for him," Philip was saying. "I rang him about an hour ago and there was no reply, then somebody answered and they looked and they said he went home and then George asked me to ring him back. If you see him could you tell him to ring me or George or preferably me. . .O.K.?"

He turned back to the Australians who were hovering in the hall. "I'm sorry. . . ."

"That's O.K.," said the director charitably. "Let's finish it off and we'll be done."

"Can I just ring George back now?" pleaded Philip. "I'm terribly sorry. He's just asked me to ring round some people. I know it's driving you up the fucking wall."

"Hurry up! I want to make a phone call," yelled Sarah.

"I'll just be two seconds," said Philip to the television men. "I'm sorry to keep you waiting. I know it's selfish but he'll start screaming at me."

He dialled and shoved a coin into the slot.

"Hello, George. Listen, he's not at Binnie's and I tried Denzil as well and Denzil was going like he didn't know it was me. Stupid bastard."

"You look fed up," said Sarah glancing at the director sympathetically.

Philip rambled on about Denzil and Marilyn, standing by the front door, his hair a mass of newspaper bows, while the Australians smoked cigarettes and studied their shoes.

"Come on, Philip, get off the bloody phone," screamed Sarah. "These people have been working all day. Hurry up. . ."

"Listen, do you want to come out to eat later?" Philip asked George. "I'll ring you back in about ten minutes."

He slammed down the receiver muttering "drives you mad". The television crew nodded in silent agreement.

Twenty minutes later the filming was finished and Philip was back on the phone to George making complicated arrangements to pick him up without allowing the driver to see where he lived.

The Australians were standing around in the hall again, waiting for a minicab to arrive, when Marilyn finally rang.

"You two are driving me up the bloody wall," said Philip. "George has been trying to get you. What are you playing at, Marilyn? He's not being evil about you – it's just you promised to ring him. Everytime he rang I said 'he wanted to speak to you, George', and he was going 'I think it's disgusting he couldn't be bothered'. It's just pathetic. It's like being at school, it really is, but, either way, dear, have you eaten?"

It was nearly midnight when Boy George and Philip Sallon finally settled down to steak and chips at the Inter-Continental Hotel at Hyde Park Corner – without Marilyn.

At approximately the same time, on the other side of London, the Australian television crew were thankfully wrapping themselves around a litre bottle of duty-free Black Label.

18

The Class of '72. Circled: George and Sharon Walker

1 "A Bit of a Torment"

George Alan O'Dowd was born on 14 June, 1961 into the uninspiring suburban sprawl of south-east London, a bleak landscape of vandalized council estates and impoverished expectations.

It was the year that Brian Epstein discovered a group called The Beatles playing in a basement club in Liverpool known as The Cavern; the beginning of an era that was to herald a revolution in fashion, music and morals. Youth and talent were about to take precedence over background and birthright in a brave new world where the old school tie was a distinct social disadvantage and a working-class accent the key to success.

London was about to swing – but not for the O'Dowd family. Not yet, at any rate.

George, the third of six children, grew up in a cramped chaotic semi-detached house on the Middle Park council estate in Eltham. He was a bright, affectionate child with a winning smile. His father, Jeremiah – Jerry to his friends – still remembers him as a tiny tot in a siren suit hurling himself out of his mother's arms to hug him when he met them off the boat-train from Dublin.

Certainly, despite terrible rows during his adolescence, George has inherited many of his father's characteristics – particularly his fiery temper.

The son of a Belfast stonemason and a mother from County Tipperary in Southern Ireland, Jerry combines a toughness bred of the necessity to survive with the inherent romanticism of his Celtic roots. His own childhood in London's arsenal suburb of

Woolwich was hard. In the late 1930s it was the Irish immigrants in Britain who were the victims of racism – a word that had yet to be invented. At school, young Jerry was isolated and abused by the other children who jeered at him for being 'a paddy' and regularly beat him up. "It's strange," confided Jerry recently to George, "how people make you into what you don't want to be."

What they made him into was a fighter. Working on the premise that if you can't join 'em, beat 'em, Jerry took secret boxing lessons so that he could at least defend himself. He already had the guts of a street scrapper, all he needed was the skills. At thirteen he was expelled from school for fighting.

From then on, boxing became his mainstay. He fought for his regiment in the army and as a civilian took the most gruelling labouring jobs in order to build up his boxing muscles. He made himself into a stereotype of all that is manly, just as George has made himself into a caricature of all that is not. But even in his dress, Jerry stayed within the boundaries of accepted rebellion. In the Teddy Boy era he wore meticulous Italian suits and pink shirts, Brylcreeming his dark hair up into a quiff. "I was a pretty wild young man," he said. "I was always asking awkward questions." He once told his Catholic priest that he was breaking God's law by not following the biblical command to "be fruitful and multiply". It was the kind of ingenuous logic at which George too has always excelled.

On his twenty-third birthday Jerry was fired from his navvying job after an ex-wrestler colleague had picked a fight with him. Despite being a virtual non-drinker Jerry went down to the pub where his sister Mary worked and met an eighteen-year-old friend of hers just off the boat from Dublin. One look into Dina Glynn's smiling Irish eyes and Jerry was hooked.

The fact that Jerry proposed to Dina soon after they met and married her against the wishes of his family and even of the local Catholic priest – all of whom thought he should at least meet her family – demonstrates both the impetuosity and rebelliousness which was to become a hallmark of his son George. Out of his own large family only his elder sister attended the wedding at St Peter's Church in Woolwich. Jerry knocked off work at midday and changed into his suit in a public toilet. His one regret was that the priest refused to marry them over the telephone.

Jerry and Dina moved into a tiny two-roomed rented flat in Plumstead which cost them £4 a week. They had nothing apart from the O'Dowd determination to succeed. Jerry took the jobs no one else wanted. At one point he decorated a complete site of brand new maisonettes single-handed, working on the outsides in daylight and the interiors at night, earning £75 for each unit.

The same year they married, 1957, their first son, Richard, was born followed at roughly two-yearly intervals by Kevin, George, Gerald, David and Siobhain. The growing family moved around from one overcrowded flat to another. When George was born they were living at Jerry's mother's house in Burrage Road, Plumstead. Their council house in Joan Crescent on Eltham's Middle Park Estate was their first proper home; but with the five boys sharing one small bedroom it soon turned into a nightmare.

Dina's pleas to the council for a bigger house were met with derision until she stopped paying the rent. Outwardly very much the traditional Irish housewife, subordinating her own life to that of her husband, Dina still possessed plenty of spirit and spunk of her own. To the local council she emerged from being yet another tiresome statistic into a force with which to be reckoned, and the family was moved to a bigger house.

George went with his mother one Saturday morning to look at the end-of-

A suburban childhood: the O'Dowds' homes in south-east London

terrace eight-roomed house on the top of Shooters Hill, just a couple of miles away from their existing home.

"Ooh, mum, it's huge!" marvelled the ten-year-old, hopping from one leg to the other in excitement. "We'll have it, we'll have it, won't we?"

Of all the boys, George and Gerald were the least compatible. Gerald took after his father as a sports and fitness fanatic. George hated anything physical and was interested in art, pop music and clothes. It was therefore curious – and for reasons she still cannot explain – that Dina should have put the two boys in a bedroom together. It was to prove an explosive combination and one that helped to drive both of them to extremes.

Already George was starting to emerge as a volatile character in his own right. Even as a small boy he knew exactly how he wanted

to dress and frequently refused to wear the clothes his mother bought for him, not conforming even to his school uniform.

In common with his brothers he had begun his education at Middle Park Primary School on the estate where they lived. There, the teachers describe the family as "caring" and George as "a nice, friendly but unremarkable little boy". His classmates remember him mainly for his singing. And for being good at art. He could draw David Bowie so well that it looked like a photograph, according to one of his fellow pupils. In fact, his love of Bowie was something he shared with a rather unconventional art teacher who used to play Bowie records during lessons. George approved of her because she allowed the children the freedom to express themselves artistically without restrictions – provided they behaved, and his skill flourished under her tuition. If her pupils were naughty she punished them by making them walk up and down the corridor balancing weights on their hands. At other times she would tell them "if you want to act like a dog you can get under the table like a dog". Destined to become an eccentric himself

George already admired it in others.

George was also in the choir and used to entertain the other children in his year to solo performances of the latest pop records when the teacher was out of the room. Even in the Cubs he sang and was always the first boy to dress up when it came to putting on

"A bit of a loner" – George in the Cubs

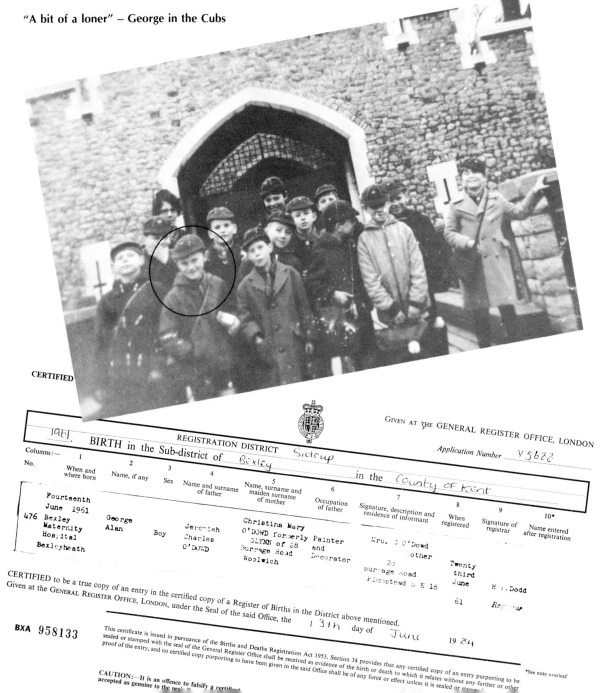

CERTIFIED

George's kid brother, Gerald

sketches. And at parties George would always be the one to get up and sing or do an act while the other children were still hiding their faces in their mothers' skirts. Yet, despite his desire to entertain – and be noticed – scout leader Mick Strevens still recalls George as being a bit of a loner. "Unlike some of the other lads he never seemed to have very many friends."

Friends or not, George was already showing the craving to compete. When he was nine he came first in both the Cub camp skipping heat and the finals of the athletics meeting – despite his dislike of games. And he earned his Bronze Arrow, awarded to cubs for a series of minor practical achievements such as being able to do simple first aid, tie knots, make a cup of tea, help around the house and do the washing-up. Even at that young age George was the most domesticated of all the boys and Gerald still remembers him polishing the family's photograph of the Queen and Princess Margaret as small children.

When the family moved to Shooters Hill, George went to the nearby Eltham Green Secondary School. Sharon Walker was the only other child who was in his class both at Middle Park and Eltham Green and remembers him as a "bit of a torment". One of his favourite tricks was to pull away the chair just as someone was about to sit down

on it. "He did it to me once and I was so angry that I got up and punched him," says Sharon. "If he wanted to borrow a ruler he'd just grab it off your desk and flick it at you before dancing back to his own desk with it. He wasn't really a show-off – just a bit out in front; not weird so much as different."

At home, George's life was becoming increasingly turbulent. He and Gerald sqabbled constantly. Their narrow bedroom was divided down the middle by two wardrobes. George painted his half of the room coffee and cream and covered the walls with posters of David Bowie and Marc Bolan. Gerald hung football and racing-car pictures on his side of the room. Since Gerald was already a keen boxer and fitness fanatic George also stuck photographs of muscle men on the walls to annoy him.

Their clashes frequently left their mark. Once, during a particularly bitter fight, George threw a tin of white emulsion paint at Gerald which his father had left lying in the hall. Gerald ducked and the paint splattered all over the brand new carpet. Horrified, George grabbed the Hoover and tried to vacuum up the wet paint. His mother arrived home to find her new carpet covered in emulsion and the Hoover ruined.

Another fight ended with George locking his brother out of the back room. Gerald hurled himself against the shut door, jettisoning the contents of the cup of coffee George was holding all over the wallpaper. For weeks afterwards their mother puzzled over the little brown spots that had appeared on the wall.

Schooldays

". . . people make you into what you don't want to be" – George's father, Jerry O'Dowd

But, while Gerald had the brawn, George had the bravado – and the quick wits and sharp tongue to go with it. He could also be infuriatingly logical, with an answer to everything, an attribute which caused constant battles both at school and home.

He was already fascinated with clothes. While his elder brother, Richard, was into the 'Clockwork Orange' look – orange boots and dungarees – George went for the gentler Marc Bolan style, dressing in embroidered jackets, cheesecloth shirts and flared trousers with velvet cut-outs. He once horrified his Sunday School teachers by turning up in a big floppy hat, platform shoes, a camel-hair coat, flared trousers and a cravat. He started going to concerts by people like David Cassidy, David Essex and, of course, David Bowie.

His theatrical garb was the classic cry for attention, possibly a reaction against what he felt was a lack of it at home. Too young to understand the pressures his parents were going through with little money and six children to support, George felt deprived of the affection he demanded. He longed for his father to cuddle him as he had when he was little but Jerry often had other things on his mind. After a hard day's work on a building site he was more likely, when he got home, to give his sons a clout round the ears than a hug. And the fact that he and George were both equally outspoken and dogmatic brought about a clash of personalities which left no room for compromise. Always a child to say what he believed in, George would answer back – particularly if he felt his father was in the wrong. Occasionally their arguments would end with Jerry chasing his stubborn son down the road. Even then George would still try to have the last word.

It was scarcely the kind of behaviour likely to lessen the chasm that had grown between father and son.

Jerry admits: "Once I got so furious with George that I smashed down the bathroom door because he was hiding behind it. I didn't want to hurt him – I just didn't know how to get through to him."

Another bone of contention in the tempestuous O'Dowd household was boxing. Jerry ran a boxing school and, remembering his own painful childhood, was determined that all his sons should learn how to defend themselves. George, however, hated anything violent and certainly did not want to be part of the macho scene to which his brother Gerald devoted himself. Even so, his father persuaded him to go down to the gym and got him skipping and punching the bag.

"The truth is that when he was little the other children would sometimes bully him and he let them get away with it," says Jerry. "He wouldn't do anything about it. He'd just cry a bit, then walk away. Even when he was tiny George was always a pacifist. So, really, I was just trying to toughen him up to make him stand up for himself. I wanted him to face his attackers." He adds: "He's a very strong boy and he used to be very handy with his fists. Let's face it – if George belted you you'd know all about it."

Yet, despite his father's faith in his pugilistic skills, none of George's friends can recall him ever defending himself with

anything other than his sharp tongue. Cross-country running was the only sport he enjoyed – he even ran for his school.

George used to argue incessantly with his mother too, once exasperating her to such an extent that she hurled the toaster at him. And the sound of crashing plates was a regular occurrence in the O'Dowd household. "I've never won an argument against George," admits Dina today. "He always has to have the last word. But, even when we rowed he would storm out the door and be back in the kitchen a minute later saying 'would you like a cup of tea?' He would flare up but then he'd calm down and forget all about it."

And, whether he was producing excuses as to why he should not go to school or reasons why he should dye his hair purple, there was never any disputing George's logic. "Usually when someone argues they come out with a right load of rubbish," says his brother Gerald. "But when you argue with George you think to yourself, 'he's right. I can understand what he's talking about'."

Even today George insists on getting his own way. "I always know when I've scored a vital hit because he says 'well, never mind about that', and changes the subject completely," says his father.

And Dina adds: "If George doesn't want to answer a question he'll talk about something you're interested in and by the time he's finished you'll have forgotten what you asked him in the first place. He never gets flustered. Even when he was a child I used to get in all of a tizzy when we argued and he'd

Mother, Dina, driven into "a tizzy" by George

say – 'that won't solve anything'."

Uncompromising and independent, George was never close to his parents as a child. "I didn't want anyone interfering in my territory," he says. Even so, he loved his father and mother and longed for them to be more demonstrative in their affection for him. An emotional child himself, he even accepted his father's occasional outbursts of anger because to George that was better than showing no emotion at all.

And, sometimes, Jerry O'Dowd's Irish temper was roused on George's behalf. Once, when George was going through a period of wearing plastic bags, he and his friend, Laura, were picked up by the police and strip-searched for drugs. George's parents were called out in the middle of the night to collect them. "I could see George's face was all bruised and I asked him who had done it," recalls Jerry. "He pointed to a large ginger-headed policeman and I was going to lay into him but my wife calmed me down." But Jerry was still incensed enough to launch an official complaint against the policeman concerned.

After the bathroom door drama, during which George tripped and cut himself – a wound which looked far worse than it actually was – he ran away from home and spent two weeks sleeping at a friend's house down the road, until his parents telephoned to get him back. And, because he still needed the support of the family structure, George went home.

Things improved after that and Jerry and George began to lay the foundations for the close relationship they share today. During George's absence, Jerry had come to terms with the fact that many of the traits that irritated him in his unruly son were the ones that George had inherited from him in the first place.

2 "Such a Poof"

*T*he first time Dina O'Dowd's Irish mother saw George in full flamboyant regalia she was horrified.

"Mother of God, Dina, you're not letting him walk out like that, are you?" she exclaimed.

Her daughter tried to placate her. "Oh, leave him be, mum, for gawd's sake," she told her. "I get enough headaches in this house as it is."

But George was not prepared to leave it at that.

"Well, what's the matter with me, nan," he demanded.

"You're a real weirdo," said his grandmother. "I don't know what your grandad would say if he could see you."

"Well, I think you dress weird, nan," retorted George to his startled grandmother, getting in the last word as usual.

The sequel to this little family episode was that George and his grandmother became great friends. "They sat and chatted and from then on if I ever told George off my mum would tell me to leave him alone," says Dina. "He seemed to wrap her round his little finger."

Certainly George's knack of being able to win over people of all ages has greatly contributed to his current success. Who would have believed that a man singer dressed up as woman, complete with flawless make-up and flowing dreadlocks could have won the God-fearing hearts of the matrons of America's mid-west?

Even as a tiny child George had the ability

George and Tracy – "basically out to shock"

to get on with people. Outgoing and unimpeded by normal childish inhibitions such as shyness, George would talk to anyone. The old ladies in the neighbourhood adored him because George helped them across the roads, carried their bags for them, did their shopping and – most important of all – took the time to chat to them.

Complete strangers frequently congratulated his parents on their "lovely-mannered boy" and once one elderly woman told Dina "I pray for that boy of yours every night because he's got such a beautiful heart."

His mother was continually astonished by the number of people who would greet George whenever she walked down the street with him. "He knew everybody," she says. He also fell for all the waifs and strays in the area, bringing a stream of ailing and maltreated children home for tea. One little girl in a wheelchair waited for him to chat to her every day after school.

Possibly it was his own yearning to be loved that made him more aware than most of other people's need for attention. But for George, the important thing was to stand out from the crowd, to be recognised as an individual, to revolt against conformity be it in thought, attitudes, behaviour or dress.

The headmaster of Eltham Green School was a strict disciplinarian, a believer in corporal punishment who had the reputation for being the toughest headmaster in Britain. To his pupils, Peter Dawson seemed like the kind of headmaster to be found within the pages of the children's comics – remote and unbending, sweeping through the corridors in flowing black gown and mortar-board, hands clasped firmly behind his back, chin in the air. Even some of the parents regarded him with a certain amount of awe.

Since his arrival in 1970 he had transformed Eltham Green from being one of the roughest schools in the area into the kind of school where even in the summer pupils could leave off their bottle green ties and

Headmaster Peter Dawson, not ". . . prepared to accept responsibility for what George might do . . ."

Eltham Green – George's occasional school

blazers only with the headmaster's permission. However, George O'Dowd had little time for what, in his opinion, were unnecessary rules and regulations. With his above-average intelligence, logical mind and lively imagination, he regarded his headmaster as a force to be not so much opposed as totally ignored. The teachers, in turn, recognised that here they had a rebel with a difference.

Peter Dawson remembers him as an "intelligent, very single-minded lad. If he made up his mind to do something, then that is what he'd do. He was a bit insular, not the sort of fellow who was in the middle of a crowd. He didn't have any close relationships with what I call the 'heavy mob', the other rebels. He was a bit too clever for them."

In fact, George spent most of his time with the girls. "They liked me because I made them laugh," he admits. "I always got the best-looking girls at school, the really pretty ones, because I was funny. I was fun to be with. They used to think I was such a poof!"

Certainly, George seemed sexually un-threatening which may well be the secret of much of his popularity among women both then and now. But it was his individuality which set him apart from the crowd.

"George stood out because he didn't care what anyone else thought of him," says Mrs Su Cankett who taught him drama from the age of eleven to thirteen. "He didn't mind what he said. His attitude was 'if I want to wear make-up I don't give a toss what anybody says. He always wanted to shock people – even the other children in his class."

And even at that tender age George was already showing the latent signs of stardom. "I used to think to myself that this guy is going to be such a character," says Mrs Cankett. "I was always convinced he was going to be something – and be unusual. Of that I was sure. Because he was so determined to make it. His attitude was always 'I'm not going to spend my life working in a shop or driving a bus or whatever.' There was always that sort of gut feeling in him.

"He was very camp, outrageous, uninhibited and a great character and I personally thought he was lovely. Smashing. I was very fond of him. He used to make everyone laugh."

The fact that he enjoyed drama and was good at it doubtlessly brought out the best in George, but even his former headmaster admits: "He did stand out. He had his own idiosyncracies, his own character, his own ideas – and he went off and did them."

At the time, however, Peter Dawson and most of his fellow teachers would have preferred George to follow their ideas a little more closely. Ironically, their opinion of him was probably much the same as his own. "I've always been obnoxious and I've always been a big-mouth," says George. "I'm quite aware that I didn't fit in. I did it deliberately because I knew it was the only way I would be relieved of that pressure of going to school." Curiously, his best subject was religious education – "I think I had a strong feeling for spiritual things," he says, and adds: "I still have" – followed by Art, English and poetry. Every other subject he considered a waste of time. "I'm one of those people who picks things up and then drops them. I wanted to do just English and Art but I had to do all the other stuff as well. I would have liked to have done music but I was never really encouraged to. The attitude was 'if you can't kick a ball – outside the class'. It wasn't a case of making you do what you're good at but of doing everything else."

More than anything, however, he wanted to be noticed – still craving the attention he felt he lacked at home. "At school I went out of my way to get more attention than anyone else," he admits. "The teacher would tell me to get up and read something out because I had a high-pitched voice and I'd turn round and say 'no, I will not' or words to that effect. I'd be rude and everyone else would laugh.

I was like a court jester."

It was around this time, in 1975, that George met Tracy Burch.

Until then, George had been dressing more or less like the other fashion-conscious kids, going through the various phases of the 1970s' fashions: short hair and GI shirts for the Glenn Miller look: flared trousers and platform heels for the Mod look. When he met Tracy he was into his David Bowie phase – pleat-fronted de-mob trousers and Tuff shoes, quite conventional for the time.

Tracy, however, had bright green and silver hair cut into a triangle with a fringe down to her nose. George was entranced.

Unbeknown to him Tracy had manufactured the meeting after seeing him in the street with his school-friend, Ruth. "I thought 'that's a nice-looking chap'," recalls Tracy. "He was terribly good-looking, very manly. And although he was dressed more or less the same as everybody else he still did look different in a way and I thought, 'ooh – he's nice'."

So she went out of her way to renew her slight acquaintance with the trusting Ruth and the next time she saw her with George she stopped for a chat.

"Hello, you old bag," said George with his customary charm. Tracy was bowled over. "I'd never met anyone like him before. I remember getting home and saying 'I've just met this bloke and he's amazing'."

The mutual attraction of Tracy's outrageous hair and George's dubious repartee proved irresistible and George left Ruth to team up with Tracy. It was the start of a friendship that influenced both their lives.

For the next few months, George and Tracy were inseparable. They urged one another on to ever wilder looks and escapades. Described by George as "my wierdest girlfriend", Tracy encouraged him to experiment with his hair and his clothes. "We were basically out to shock people because it's such fun when you're young," says Tracy.

She was thirteen, a year younger than George, and the second of three daughters of the co-owner of a sheet paper mill. Her mother worked in a fabric shop which meant that she was able to bring home odd bits of material for Tracy and George to run up. The rest of the time they scoured the local Oxfam shops for the most outlandish cast-offs they could find.

Charity begins at Oxfam – haute couture on the house

Although the clothes cost virtually nothing, George on principle always made a big fuss about the prices. "What do you think this is – Harrods?" he would demand cheekily of the shop assistant, holding up a tuxedo several sizes too large for him priced at fifty pence. A huge row would ensue, ending up with Tracy shoving the coat into her bag out of sight of the assistant.

"George would be loving it but the shop lady would be getting quite upset so I used to say 'to save problems, I'll get it'," says Tracy.

"We used to steal most of the stuff. We'd make sure we both had loose clothes on and we'd go into the changing rooms and put on about six pairs of trousers and skirts and jumpers and then our own clothes over the top.

"Some days we'd go around every Oxfam shop in a six-mile radius and steal enough clothing to last us a month."

George's teasing was not restricted to hapless shop assistants. Tracy came in for her share, too. Trying on a pair of shoes she would ask George's opinion.

"They're lovely, they're lovely. Get them,

George making a fashion point

Tracy," he would tell her. Then, outside the shop after she had bought them he would say: "I don't know how you could buy them. They're fucking horrible."

"I always fell for it," says Tracy ruefully.

They would take the clothes home, rip them up, dye them, redesign them and stitch them together on their mothers' sewing machines. Imagination was everything – the wilder, the better. Once they got a pair of frilly shirts from Oxfam, dyed one red, one green, cut them in half and sewed the opposite sides together to make identical jester tops.

They spent hours wandering along Chelsea's trendy King's Road, posing for the benefit of the passers-by, studying the most striking of the mid-1970s fashions and rushing home to make them up themselves for a fraction of the cost. Their favourite shop was Acme Attractions in the Chelsea Antique Market, the inspiration for their fur fabric monkey suits with huge padded shoulders tipped with long white spikes. They copied the latest baggy trousers with transparent plastic pockets or adorned with bits of elastic and zips up the sides, and bought themselves plastic sandals which they wore with luminous socks.

George's parents were appalled. "They thought I was a terrible exhibitionist and that I was leading him astray," admits Tracy. "His mother was always worrying about what the neighbours would think." What the neighbours *did* think is largely unprintable.

George and Tracy started staying away from school, rummaging through the Oxfam shops instead, or going for long walks over Blackheath Common. George sang constantly, mainly Bowie numbers. ". . . give me your heart and I'll love you till Tuesday," he would serenade Tracy beside Blackheath's Folly Pond.

Dressed like twins in tight drainpipe trousers with their jester tops and cat sunglasses curving up at the sides, they attracted the stares, sniggers and insults of

"I've got the guts to wear it – they haven't"

astonished passers-by. "We didn't mind at all," says Tracy, "it was such fun. People would take the mickey out of us all the time but George was so good at talking them down that it would leave them shattered – and speechless."

They discovered joss sticks and George bought a dozen packets and lit them all at the same time. The heavy scent of jasmine wafting through the house did little to improve his mother's over-worked sense of humour.

At the beginning of their friendship Tracy made no secret of the fact that she fancied George, but he made it plain that he was not interested in anything other than a brother-sister relationship. Once or twice Tracy tried putting her arms around her new boyfriend. "Don't be bloody stupid, you silly little tart," snapped George, shaking her off. And whenever she said anything affectionate to him he would respond equally un-romantically – "shut up, you silly old cow." It was not rudeness so much as shyness that made George react so strongly – as he still does when he feels a situation is beyond his control. Tracy realised that if the relationship was to continue it would have to be on George's platonic terms.

Tracy lived in New Eltham, two bus rides away from George's house. When he came to pick her up he would usually be several hours late. Then he would refuse to go anywhere unless he had something to eat first – usually in the order of eggs, bacon, sausage and baked beans. "He was such a pig," says Tracy, a term frequently used by George's friends describing his eating habits. "He could eat everything and anything. I'd just sit there watching him eat and then when he was ready to go I had to be ready, too." Certainly, the quantity George can consume and the speed at which he can devour it is more suited to his six-foot frame than to his meticulously made-up face and elegant gowns. But that, too, stems from his inherent need for the love and attention he felt he was lacking as a child.

Tracy remembers sitting with him in Wimpy Bars while George ordered four milk shakes at a time, drinking them one after the other, loudly gurgling them down through the straw to the very last drop. "Then he would gobble his food as fast as possible so he could start on mine. I'd be lucky to get a few mouthfuls down before he'd scoffed the lot."

One evening she and George went for a hamburger at McDonalds in nearby Woolwich. They were dressed for the occasion in leg warmers, short jackets and flat caps – "like we were going out shooting". The manager took one look at their get-up and threw them out. "We don't want any trouble," he shouted after them. "We're not having punk rockers in here."

Dressed up in their latest finery, plastered with spray-on silver and gold glitter with feather earrings and feathers in their hair, they would go to the discos in Woolwich to dance to the imported soul records, drink Coca-Cola and show themselves off. They always stood out from the other kids who were still in flared trousers or baggy shirts and jeans. And, wherever they went, Tracy usually paid. "George never seemed to have any money," she says. "I suppose he must have spent it all on records."

The St Peter's was one of their favourite haunts, a seedy little basement soul club charging about ten pence admission, where they could dance around to their favourite records such as *Rigamortis* and *Open Sesame*. When George eventually stopped going there, the manager rang up his mother to find out where he was. "Tell Georgie to come back," he told her, "this place is dead without him."

One of George's more astonishing outfits was a pair of large white baggy trousers covered in yellow spots with a black top with a white spot on it joined by a wide cummerbund. "He looked just like a clown," says his mother. "It used to amaze me how he got his hair to stand up on end."

"Don't you mind people laughing at you?" Dina once asked him.

"No," said George. "I don't care. Let them take the mickey – I've got the guts to wear it, they haven't"

But dressing up was not all fun. Although George and Tracy did everything they could to be noticed, often the attention they got was rather more than either of them bargained for. Their most frightening moments usually occurred on their way home from the regular Wednesday night disco at the Woolwich Town Hall. They would frequently share the last bus to Eltham with crowds of black youths mostly two or three years older than themselves and raring for a fight.

"They couldn't understand why George looked so poofy," says Tracy.

George used to have to get off the bus first but often the youths would make him stay on until their stop. "George used to be petrified," says Tracy, "and so did I. We'd go back to Eltham and they would really hit him. And I'd have to stick up for him. There was me trying to get him away from them and trying to attract other people's attention."

Once, after a disco, a black gang picked on George because they said he was wearing nail varnish on his toes. The bus was full so we had to go upstairs," says Tracy, "and the youths started hurling abuse at George, calling him a poof and this, that and the other. When we got to Eltham they started punching him in the stomach and calling him nasty names. I was trying to hit them and trying to drag George away and screaming at the top of my voice. In the end they got scared because I was making such a row and they left him but he was crying and he was in a state and he had been hurt. He was quite a softy in those days even though he had such a hard exterior.

"It was terrifying, really nasty. I saw George on to his bus and he got home all right and the next day he'd forgotten all about it and didn't seem to care at all."

It was this ability to forget – if not forgive – that enabled George to keep going when

Tracy persuaded George to experiment with his hair

less dedicated exhibitionists might have packed it in and crept back into their tee-shirts and jeans. Besides, he believed in what he was doing and George O'Dowd had no intentions of discarding his convictions just because a handful of thugs did not like the way he looked. So, for the next few months, beatings-up were to become a way of life.

On one occasion his father went down to the St Peter's Club himself to confront a black youth who had been hasselling George for some time. Jerry pulled the bully to one side and told him: "It's not a good thing to throw your weight around in that manner. You think you're tough but you're not really." Many years later he met the youth, now a professional boxer, at the divisional boxing championships. "How's George getting on?" enquired the lad, and admitted: "I used to pick on him because I thought he was weird but he can look down and laugh at me now, can't he!"

But for most of the time George defended himself with his tongue, lashing out at his antagonisers with a practised mixture of bitchiness and bravado.

It was Tracy who first persuaded George to colour his hair and change the style, and got him interested in make-up. "Some nights I'd be playing around with my little sister and her friends, putting make-up on their faces, and George would put a bit on himself and it would be all over the place. I used to say 'why don't you wear a bit of blusher or a bit of eyeliner to make your eyes stand out a bit more?' and he'd say – 'I'll see, I'll see' but I don't think he could be bothered."

And he certainly did not approve of Tracy wearing too much make-up herself. "He used to criticise my make-up all the time, telling me how to put it on and I'd say 'what the hell do you know?' and he'd grab my face and try to do it for me." If they were going to a party, with Tracy trying to get as much on her face as possible George would say "Oh – you look a right state. Who do you think you are with all that shit on your face?"

George could be unkind in other ways, too. Tracy remembers tottering along the King's Road in excrutiatingly high winkle-pickers that were "killing" her. "George was making me walk everywhere and I was nearly in tears, saying 'I can't go any further, George'. And he was saying 'Get up and bloody well walk. I want to do this and I want to do that' and he made me limp around for hours."

For a time George had a part-time evening job washing glasses at the Tiger's Head pub in Chislehurst. While he was there he always made a point of stacking up all the empty soda syphons outside the back door. Then, after he had finished work, he and Tracy would shin over the fence and steal the syphons.

"It was always down to me to take them into an off-license," recalls Tracy, "while George would be outside hiding. We went round all the off-licenses in Chislehurst and I'd tell them my dad had had a party. They knew I was up to something but they always paid up – seventy-five pence for each syphon. We made quite a few bob like that."

But while his evenings were proving both profitable and – for the most part – pleasurable, George's schooldays were neither. The problem was not so much his clothes, although he had been sent home once for wearing outsize platform shoes bought, ironically, by his mother in Petticoat Lane – "I thought 'if you want to wear all these ridiculous things, get on with it'," says Dina. Nor was it his constantly-changing hair – despite the red food colouring turning his white shirt collars pink when it rained. No, it was simply his blatant refusal to work, to accept any kind of authority and, increasingly, even to go to school at all, that created an untenable situation for his teachers.

"George did not fit in and did not want to," says his headmaster. "He wasn't unpopular. He was just regarded as different from other people and he did not like the fact that you had to behave and work. He hated discipline and was a perpetual truant, more skilful at playing hookey than any pupil I have ever known. He would not come to school and he would not work when we got him there."

Finally, George was transferred to the school's Special Needs Department – nicknamed The Greenhouse, an isolated classroom at the top of the school which was run by a master with experience of difficult children. "Even there he had to be watched all the time," says Peter Dawson. "If he asked to leave the classroom that would be the last you saw of him."

George responded typically by doing his best to annoy the master in charge of the sanctuary unit, insulting him and refusing to do anything. He stayed away more and more, playing truant with Tracy or just spending the days sitting in the woods by himself – often for eight hours at a time just indulging in his fantasy world. If nothing else it taught him to appreciate his own company. "Even now I love being on my own for at least three or four hours a day," he says.

The crunch came when George turned up late for school one Monday morning and bumped straight into the headmaster who had seen him in the High Street the previous Friday when he should have been at school, recognising him by his conspicuous newly-bleached hair. Threatened with a caning, George once again defied authority and told his headmaster he had had enough of school and wanted to go home.

The headmaster granted his wish by suspending him.

In the official letter dated 29 September, 1976, notifying George's parents of his decision, Peter Dawson wrote: ". . . I do not feel prepared to accept responsibility for what George might do to himself or to others if he remains on these premises. . ." The final paragraph of the letter read: "I am giving George this letter to bring home by hand but I am also sending several other copies in different ways to make sure that at least one gets through to you. I am doing this because Mrs O'Dowd told us recently that she had received none of the letters sent from the school last term. . ."

His mother went with him to see the school staff. In front of them she asked George whether he wanted to go back to school. When he said "no", Dina took him home.

So ended the state's efforts to give George a conventional education. Says George in his own defence: "I wasn't always an eccentric but if I felt something was unjustified I'd say so. And I'd give a good reason. It's obviously easier to teach twenty people who think the same than nineteen who do and one who doesn't."

With the benefit of hindsight Peter Dawson admits: "George wasn't unique in turning away from school at that age. In fact, I think it was probably a good thing for everybody that he cleared off." And, of his wayward pupil's subsequent success he says: "What has struck me is that George has been thoroughly consistent. He is still highly idiosyncratic. Even within the pop scene he's different. I think that's his most important characteristic. Whatever everybody else is doing he's probably going to be doing something different."

For George the whole experience served as an important lesson because it proved what he had always suspected – that the system is there to be beaten. He now knew that he could refuse to conform and get away with it, that survival does not necessarily depend on sticking to the rules. "Most children," says George, "fantasize about being a pilot or a football star but when they reach the age of sixteen reality hits them and they realize that they've got to work. I wasn't that kind of child. I avoided reality. I tried to create a completely different image."

Without at least the occasional routine of school to share he and Tracy began seeing each other less and less. George made new friends and his life started to revolve around London's West End. He wrote to Tracy occasionally, jokey letters that showed he had not changed. "Say 'hello' to your camp daddy and touch his knee for me," he scribbled cheekily in one of them. Still an inveterate letter writer, even on paper George is never at a loss for words.

The last time Tracy met him was in Studio 21, a club off Oxford Street. "George was wearing a long frock, a black wig down to his bum, a straw hat and he had false eyelashes and beautiful long nails," says Tracy. "He looked absolutely fabulous, like a Spanish señorita. The only thing that looked odd was the two pints of lager he was holding."

George turned round. "Hello," said Tracy.

"You haven't answered my fucking letter, you old bag," said George.

"We didn't talk much," recalls Tracy, "because he was with this really outrageous boy called Martin and George kept looking round all the time, watching what Martin was doing."

In those early, formative years both George and Tracy had a lasting effect on each other's personalities. "He contributed a lot

to me growing up," admits Tracy. "He made me more out-going and more fun." And, in return, it was Tracy who first showed George the risky delights of dressing up and being outrageous.

"Now I look at George's pictures in the newspapers or on television and I think he looks tremendous," says Tracy. "I'm so proud of him, it reduces me to tears sometimes. I knew he would be somebody one day. I couldn't see him working in a shop or being a lawyer or something like that. He was too outrageous. When I see him now I always think – I knew he'd do it and he's done it and I think he's wonderful."

The Arnolds achieve local celebrity in the Kentish Independent – October 1976

New fashion trend comes in at Black Prince d

WAY OUT IN
BEXLEY – IT
THE ARNOL

Why bother with diamond-studded ear-rings when a safety pin will do just as well — and might also be useful in an emergency? K3014

3 "Lots of Lovely Hugs and Cuddles"

*T*he Black Prince was a large, rambling Bass Charrington public house standing on an island in the middle of the London to Dover arterial road. Since the early 1960s it had featured live bands in its ballroom, first traditional jazz artists like Acker Bilk and Kenny Ball, then the avant-garde heroes of pop such as Rod Stewart, Long John Baldry, Eric Clapton and Georgie Fame. By the mid-1970s the bands had become too expensive and their equipment too extensive to be practical and the management transformed the ballroom into a twice-weekly discotheque.

It was the pre-punk period when the kids were casting around for something new to capture their imagination. They found themselves in a cultural limbo with just a few straggling hippies and a handful of complacent musicians left over from the 1960s to call their own. With nothing really original to excite them the fashions tended back towards the 1940s and 1950s and the music towards Glenn Miller and Bryan Ferry. A few cultural islands such as Wigan Casino produced their own excitement but in most places there was little more than a smattering of soul clubs playing funky black music while everyone waited for something to happen.

This time the rumblings of something big came not from the big cities like London and Liverpool but from behind the neat net curtains of suburbia. And, while the 1960s revolution had been a working-class one, this time it cut right across the class barriers. Everyone was bored.

It started slowly, in odd little pockets of south-east England, and it began to be noticed in suburban discotheques like the Lacy Lady in Ilford, the Roundacre in Basildon, the Goldmine on Canvey Island, the Oldfield in Northolt, the Circus Tavern in Purfleet and, of course, the Black Prince in Bexley Heath. It was not so much a fashion as an anti-fashion, an open rejection of all the traditional values associated with dressing up. Kids started gearing their appearance to appal rather than appeal, going to extraordinary lengths to make themselves as ugly and outrageous as possible. Imagination and ingenuity counted for more than hard cash – which was just as well since nobody had much of that anyway.

And, unlike their flower-clutching pot-smoking predecessors, these kids were individuals. It was not enough to shock everyone else, they wanted to shock each other as well, to stand out from even their own crowd, to be acclaimed independently – if only as objects of ridicule. Forget Aquarius. This was the age of the freak.

They assembled at the Black Prince every Thursday night, pouring in from miles around, queueing patiently in their flamboyant costumes to pay their fifty pence to get into the discotheque. Some of them rubbed gravel from the coach-park on to their chins in the hope that the "stubble" would disguise the fact that they were way under age.

And, of the couple of hundred or so youngsters who squeezed into the ballroom, certain groups of regulars stood out, a little more outgoing, a little more outrageous than the rest. Among them were Terry, Lennie and Jane, three extroverts who, with George,

Hiding his nose for fashion – George with fellow Arnold, Susan

were to form the hard core of what was to become the Bexley contingent.

Of the four, Terry's family was the most affluent. His father had his own interior design business and they lived in a five-bedroomed detached house in Erith. Terry, the second of three children, had his own horse, paid for by his parents on the understanding that he would stay at school to take his 'A' levels. Yet, not even his father's own artistic streak – which, according to Terry, allowed for certain eccentricities – could cope with his youngest son going out in the evening in a see-through florescent nylon jump suit, with lopsided hair and blusher on his cheeks.

Lennie's background was the closest to George's own. Also the son of a builder and the fifth of seven children, Lennie was brought up in a red-brick terraced council house in Welling. A good-looking, sensitive, artistic boy he was the school gymnastics champion and talented at sculpture. He was also fascinated by fashion and his mother and sisters often consulted him over their own choice of clothes. His own taste in outrage was slightly less wild than that of his friends. Even so, he wore rubber or leather jackets and bondage trousers and at one time took to going out in morning dress complete with tailcoat and pin-striped trousers. But, being a trainee hairdresser, he mostly concentrated his artistic flair on his head. He once had a big 'V' cut in the back of it and dyed red, white and blue. On other occasions it would be rainbow-coloured or bright red, flecked with black.

Jane's family lived in a three-bedroomed bungalow on a 1950s housing estate in Bexley. Her father was the import-export manager of an engineering firm and she had one brother, four years younger, who was into classical music and entirely contemptuous of his sister's idiosyncratic style of dress. Even her mother used to weep when she watched her teenage daughter walk down the street dressed in a florescent orange plastic dustbin bag with bizarre make-up and a red arrow dyed into her blackened hair.

At the Black Prince these young exhibitionists came into their own. Here they could preen and be seen. The music was loud, the dancing frenetic, the competition intense. It was the first time George had found himself in an environment in which he could excel without compromise.

The latest dance was The Bump, a vigorous routine seemingly consisting of press-ups and splits. No one drank much, just a beer or Coke. Lennie introduced the boys to lager and black-currant juice, the bright pink foam frequently matching the colour of their hair. It was suitably camp and became George's favourite drink.

The four became regular playmates. George was 14, Terry 15, and Jane and Lennie 17. By nature the most cautious, when it came to dressing up Jane was the wildest of them all. Along with the rest of the Bexley contingent – The Arnolds, as they became known, for reasons none of them can quite recall – they competed to see who could be the most outrageous, spending every spare moment at the Oxfam shops and jumble sales, buying up anything that was loud, ugly and cheap, creating their own version of street fashion. They found old crimpolene dresses and cut them short, cere tops and simulated leather skirts. They wore odd socks – the odder, the better, and stiletto heels – especially the boys. They went through a beach party phase wearing vivid Hawaiian shirts, white Bermuda shorts and short white socks and shoes. Someone invented the tabard – a white sheet stiched up the sides with black string – and the following week the Black Prince was full of them. As soon as they started a fashion they discarded it, going on to something else even more extreme. One of Jane's friends, Andrea, proved herself to be a one-woman traffic hazard, tottering along the pavement

Lager and blackcurrent and polka dots for George – already standing out from the crowd

in a string vest, skin-tight red plastic hot-pants, fishnet stockings and red stiletto shoes. George threatened to steal a straight-jacket from the local mental hospital to dress up in. And once they all went out in pyjamas and nightdresses, complete with slippers and teddy bears. When outsiders assumed they were going to a fancy dress party they were highly offended. In common with all cult leaders they took themselves very seriously indeed. They judged everyone by what they wore and were as contemptuous of the people who dressed normally – wallies, as they became known – as were the wallies of them.

In fact, George and his friends were so accustomed to being abused themselves because of the way they looked that they started hitting out first, insulting strangers who stared at their extraordinary outfits.

It was the most basic form of bravado, a rebellion against the whole stifling suburban mentality and life-style. "People hated you to dress like that," says Andrea. "They really couldn't understand it. And, in a way, we couldn't either. It was just a gut feeling but it taught us to stick up for ourselves.

"If you were extrovert you could prove you were extrovert. You could suddenly say – 'look at me. I'm not like you lot. I'm not going to spend the rest of my life going nowhere. I'm going to be something else'." And, to George in particular, that mattered more than anything else in the world.

There was the added attraction of being able to make yourself sexually ambiguous. Many of the boys who were afraid of admitting their still-latent homosexuality could hide behind their exotic clothes, while the girls were able to discard their own stereotyped roles aimed at finding a steady boyfriend and settling down with a three-piece suite and a washing machine. As one of the Bexley girls explained: "I wanted to have men friends who weren't just trying to knock me off."

And, most of all, they remember the warm camaraderie that existed between them – "lots of lovely hugs and cuddles" as Jane puts it, despite the fact that they never talked about anything except "clothes, going out and who we got off with".

When, years later, they met up again they discovered that they knew absolutely nothing about each other. But, at the time, these superficial narcissistic relationships suited them fine. "We were all of us supreme posers, supreme exhibitionists," admits Terry. "We just loved people looking at us." And George, of course, loved it more than any of them. "George adored being looked at – whether it was adoringly or nastily," says Jane. "He lapped it all up." And if there was a photographer around, George would demand to have his picture taken and make sure he got a copy of the photo.

Already tall for his age, George was considerably more mature than the average fourteen-year-old. He seldom wore much make-up in those days but experimented constantly with his naturally brown hair. And his hyper-energy tended to cause problems which even his best friends never told him about. Instead, they jokingly sprayed deodorant behind his back when he was not looking. He was also extremely camp with a very effeminate voice which worried the parents of some of his friends. "Why are you going around with him? He's homosexual," Jane's mother used to tell her and Jane, practical as ever, would reply: "I'm much safer with a homosexual than I am with an ordinary heterosexual guy".

The others looked up to Jane because she was older and, working in a bank, she earned money. Despite her calculated flamboyance she seemed almost grown up. She also mothered them all, taking them under her multi-coloured wing and worrying about them continually, especially George "who was really young and silly. Although we were all young and sillyish we weren't quite as young and silly as him."

Having found their fashion feet – and each

No 4339

LOUISE

This portion must be retained while on these premises and produced on request.

61. POLAND ST. LONDON, W.1.

Tel. 437 1693

Sleazy decadence and day trips: George on the gay club circuit and an outing to Margate for the Arnolds with Andrea (far left) and Jane (far right)

other – the Bexley contingent headed for the low lights of London. At Global Village, underneath the arches of Charing Cross Station, they met up with the rival groups from the other suburbs, all of them getting a first taste of big city nightlife. It was the Bromley contingent, led by Siouxsie (of the Banshees) and Billy Idol (of Generation X) who first discovered Louise's.

In those days there were not many places that would accept these exotically-plumed youngsters. Even the Black Prince made them take the safety pins out of their ears before letting them in. Only the gay clubs, already

catering for a much maligned minority, were unconventional enough to welcome their under-age custom.

Louise's was primarily a lesbian haunt, a dingy club in Soho's Poland Street run by the peroxided Madame Louise who sat by the door draped in furs and jewellery complete with beauty spot, long black eyelashes and gushing French accent. There was a small dance floor with an antiquated sound system but both the music and the dancing was irrelevant. Louise's was primarily a place to show yourself off. Here, in an atmosphere of sleazy 1930s-style decadence, the young egotists congregated every Friday night to massage each other's vanity among the hookers, transvestites and transsexuals who frequented the club, and rub shoulders with the embryo punk celebrities like the Sex Pistols, the Jam, the Clash, and Chelsea.

It was hardly the kind of place to take your parents and that, of course, was part of the attraction. "You knew that if your mother saw the sort of situation you were in she would murder you," says Terry. "And that was wonderful, absolutely wonderful."

George's mother was particularly concerned about the dangers awaiting him in London by night, always having been scared of the city herself. She had a talk with him about the dangers of drink, drugs and sex and made him promise to tell her if he was staying out late. Even so, George was the only one of the boys who dared to leave home actually wearing his evening attire. His parents were already used to his outrageous clothes. Lennie and Terry, on the other hand, wore big black coats over their outfits and carried bags full of accessories to be put together on the train.

And those train journeys up to Charing Cross were adventures in themselves. George and his friends seldom bothered to buy tickets, maybe just one between all of them to be handed in and argued over at the barrier while the rest of the party rushed past. Or else they would buy tickets for one stop only and bluff their way at the other end. Going home they waited until their train was about to leave and dashed through the barrier before the ticket collector realised what was happening, jumping off the train when it slowed down before reaching their station.

No one had much money in those days but it never seemed to matter. Apart from the £3 necessary to get into Lousie's everything else was free – the way George and his friends played it, anyway. Besides avoiding train fares, they stole other people's drinks at the clubs or found empty glasses and filled them

with ice. They even managed to catch the odd taxi and escape paying the fare by running like hell when they reached their destination. But mostly they would travel by foot thinking nothing of walking from Charing Cross to Camden Town for a party.

On the train into town they provided a constant source of entertainment for the other passengers who also doubtlessly presumed they were going to a fancy dress party. Sometimes they transformed the carriage into a hairdressing salon, spraying each other with cans of paint. "It was terribly camp and great fun," recalls Terry. "We'd go up to a few ladies and ask them if we could borrow their hair spray – in frightfully camp voices. We had the whole coach in hysterics."

For the boys, being camp was part of the image and, as always, it was George who excelled at it. Of them all, he was the only one who openly admitted to being gay. "We were all of us very very screwed up about our sexuality," admits Terry. "I think, in a way, dressing up was a form of escape."

And Jane remembers: "George was very proud of the fact that he was gay and I think that was probably his form of rebellion. He went on about it all the time. It was his favourite subject." Even in those early days and at that young age George stood out from the rest of the crowd. "George was never ever ordinary," remembers another of Louise's regulars. "He was always a bit of an exception."

Down in the red gloom of Louise's mirrored basement the atmosphere was

heavy with sex of one kind or another. In the words of one of the West London contingent: "It was like a party at somebody's house with people getting off with each other regardless of what sex they were. Everyone used to smoke and take drugs and anything went. Servicemen crashed out in corners, businessmen came down as voyeurs and we all used to pinch their drinks and fags. Often you couldn't get into the loo – we all used the Gents – because of the people doing things to each other." Lesbians smooched together in the alcoves and once Andrea, who was the same age as George, spotted her school games' mistress kissing another woman.

The blatant debauchery made Louise's all the more exciting to the youngsters up from the suburbs. They were scarcely prudes anyway and this was a place to have fun. There was an element of competition, too, that was not restricted purely to their dress.

Jane recalls the 24-year-old singer with one of the leading punk groups who went down to Louise's. "All the girls fancied him and we all wanted to get off with him but in the end George did. We were so fed up. We were all crazy about this guy and George just comes along and gets off with him. It happened often, actually, but I was quite upset about that particular one." On another night, the same singer invited both Terry and a girlfriend back to his flat. The pair made their excuses and fled.

"George had a very boyish and attractive face and he used to get picked up by other boys quite a lot," says Jane. "He used to like to talk about it. He was quite proud of the fact. He tried to make us jealous by talking about who he'd got off with because we wouldn't always get off with somebody and he quite often would. He often made me jealous because we tended to like the same guys and they would often turn out to be gay."

George's bragging was done largely to impress his friends but on one occasion Jane got her revenge on him. "We used to really fancy Billy Idol but George was always saying I'd never manage it. But I did. I got off with him. I really ribbed George for ages about that. I thought – O.K., I'm going to get my own back after all the times he's got off with all the guys I like."

But, despite their continual bantering, Jane admits that at times she was concerned about George. "I used to worry about him being picked up by older men, really older men. He never was but the thought of it bothered me, disgusted me in a way. I was worried about what might happen to him because he was so young. I never mentioned it to him – there was no point. It would probably have had totally the opposite effect on him."

It was not really a danger because George, like his other young gay friends at the time, was more into the visual than the physical. In that narcissistic atmosphere, looks were everything. And none of them was searching for a father figure. "Oooh – that looks good," they would hiss to one another, summing up the available talent. Or "isn't that cute!" Never – "that looks horny" or "that looks sexy". They might go off for a one-night stand but it would have to be with someone they found attractive.

And George, like everyone else at Louise's, was intent on enjoying himself. Not by nature a promiscuous person he was still experimenting with life. "He was a dreadful, dreadful flirt," says Terry, "but I think he did it mainly to shock. He loved shocking people. A lot of one-night standing went on – mainly because most of the people there were too young to get really seriously involved."

George himself admits that he slept around when he was young. "Everybody, no matter how puritanical, sleeps with a person just for sex at some stage in their life."

The regular cabaret act at Louise's was a singing/dancing duo called Biddy and Eve. Biddy had bleached white hair and wore

... keeping abreast of fashion ...

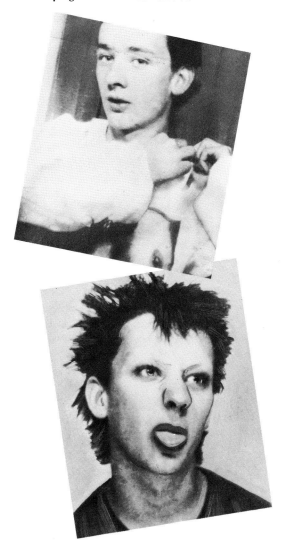

George as a matinee idol . . .

glitter on his teeth; Eve was a luscious buxom lass with a mane of hair piled on top of her head and decorated with orchids. She wore daring skin-tight frocks which plunged dramatically emphasising her remarkable frontage. George always seemed slightly envious when Biddy and Eve were in the limelight although he never mentioned it.

Late one night, when the room was crowded, Eve pulled George on to her lap, at the bar, and together they sang "We're having a heatwave". Only George's immediate friends paid any attention but they remember him being uncharacteristically shy despite covally holding his ground.

At Louise's the Bexley contingent did their own thing. And, according to Jane, nobody bothered if one of their party was missing when it was time to leave. "If George vanished we wouldn't wait for him – and vice versa. Although we all went together we wouldn't necessarily worry if we weren't together at the end. We'd look around for anyone who was missing but if he or she wasn't there we'd go."

The journeys home were long, uncomfortable and frequently frightening. Louise's shut at around 4am and George and his friends would usually sneak on to a stationary train to try to get some sleep until the 7.30 milk train was ready to leave. If they heard a guard coming they would crouch behind crates in the goods car or hurtle from carriage to carriage until they had given him the slip. Sometimes it was so freezing in the compartment that they would literally cry, huddling together for warmth, swearing they would never ever do it again although, of course, they always did. Sometimes, just to add to their discomfort they set off the fire extinguishers and sprayed each other with icy water or covered one another with shaving foam "for fun". And even in their moments of utter misery George would sing, re-writing oldies in his head. "Show me the way to my abode, I'm fatigued and I want to retire. . ." and everybody would join in the chorus. "He

. . . and putting on the Sid Vicious style

was always the one who kept the troops happy," says Jane, "always the one who tried to tell us that it wasn't so bad after all. He very much wanted everyone to be happy." And Terry agreed: "There were times when if George hadn't been around I would have died." For breakfast, Jane always handed out bowls of cereal or biscuits which she had been carrying in one of the endless plastic bags and little straw suitcases which accompanied them all wherever they went.

Getting to the station could also be a problem – dressed as they were and with George in tow. For despite his reluctance to fight back he seemed to take positive pleasure in baiting the Teddy Boys who were already the sworn enemies of the kids with the pre-Punk look. Once, walking through Leicester Square in the early hours of the morning George, Jane and Terry spotted a gang of about thirty Teds coming towards them.

"Let's go round the back way," suggested Terry sensibly, instead of which George started shouting abuse at the Teds. There was a glint of steel as the gang prepared for action. George, Jane and Terry did not wait to find out what that action might be. "I've never run so fast in my life," recalls Terry. "I was terrified. But George throught it was the funniest thing. They came at us in hot pursuit and we ran like hell. I can still remember hurling my feet across that bloody bridge by Big Ben. We must have run at a hundred miles an hour, we were going like the clappers. And those Teddy Boys, if they'd got us, would have ripped us to pieces, I know. But then we just fell down in a heap of exhaustion and laughed and laughed and laughed. It was hysterical."

Running away from Teds had become a fairly regular occurrence in George's life. His painful experiences at the hands of the local louts during his time with Tracy Burch had impressed upon him the value of showing a clean pair of heels, albeit stiletto ones. Yet, he loved dicing with danger and was unable to resist baiting his potential aggressors. Walking along the King's Road on a Saturday afternoon with Jane he teased the Teds along the way.

"Thank God Elvis is dead!" he taunted, while the ever-cautious Jane held her breath and prayed. "Oh George, shut up. You are stupid – be careful!" she muttered but not loud enough for George to hear.

The King's Road was still the venue for Saturdays, where the kids from all the different areas would congregate, posing on the pavement and stealing the latest fashion ideas displayed in the shop windows. The Chelsea Antique Market was still a favourite haunt too, where the stalls sold all that was weird and wonderful and up-to-date. And it was there that Jane and George got to know Troy Morris, a Jamaican musician who had opened a clothes stall called 'Shades'.

By now the media had latched on to the way that the kids in the clubs were dressing and had labelled the bizarre new look "Punk". And, with the media attention, came the backlash of violence, the much-hyped puking, spitting and kicking that became self-fulfilling, complete anathema to the original concept that had been created largely by the peace-loving gay contingent. Even so, suddenly Punk was in.

Troy, a drummer by profession, had no experience of the fashion business and welcomed any advice he could get. George and Jane had plenty to offer. They had, after all, been among the originators of this weird new look and Troy realised that whatever they wore today, the kids in the street would be buying tomorrow.

So the three friends spent hours sprawled on the floor of Troy's cluttered stall, armed with cans of spray paint, decorating the second-hand clothes that Troy bought from jumble sales and junk shops, inserting a zip here, a cut there, adding safety-pins, even beer cans, changing styles and colours, ripping hems, tie-dyeing and basically doing all the things they had always done for

A page from history – courtesy of "Punk Rock" with Philip Sallon second from right

themselves anyway. They experimented by spraying paint through barbed wire to produce a spiky pattern around the necks of t-shirts. Jane showed Troy the outfits she and George had made out of shocking pink and black fur fabric and he asked them to make some more for him to sell.

When George left school, Troy employed him for £6 a day, utilizing both George's flair for design and his natural ability to sell anything, especially himself. It was to be an eye-opener for George whose world had been fairly limited until now. Today, he says of his time working with Troy: "It changed my life. Dealing with people made me confident. I got out of my silly little environment and began to meet middle-class people and see what a different world it was. I always thought people who were rich acted differently but I found out they were just as disgusting." Troy respected George's quicksilver tongue and ricochet humour. Once, when George was hanging up some clothes on the rail, someone threw the customary insults at him. Without even stopping what he was doing George riposted right on cue. "It was like the second line of a song," says Troy. "The wit was so instant that the two complemented each other even though they were being insulting."

George was wearing make-up now, nothing overdone – just a bit of lipstick, some eyeliner, a few highlights. When Troy demanded "shit, man, what are you doing with all that make-up?" George capitalized on his skill of being able to relate any rationalization to the person he was addressing. "Look at Little Richard and James Brown," he told Troy. "They wear make-up. Look at those Indians covered in war-paint. That's make-up." Troy was convinced. "I thought 'sure, it makes sense'. I couldn't knock it. I could see the logic in it."

At that time, the King's Road had become a weekly battleground for the Punks, the Teds, the Skinheads and the police. To confuse them all, George made himself up half Punk, half Ted, his hair pink on one side and greased into a quiff on the other. On one half of his body he wore tartan, on the other a draped jacket and drainpipe trouser leg. "Nobody knew what he was at," chuckles Troy. "The Teds wanted to kill him, the Punks wanted to kill him, the Skins wanted to kill him and the football crowd wanted to kill him."

On Saturday afternoon Shades would do a roaring trade in raincoats which the Punks bought to disguise themselves from the Teds who were chasing them. It was also a regular venue for magazine photographers hoping, among other things, to get a few shots of George in his latest outfit. George, naturally,

"George was never ordinary"

posed willingly and loved the attention.

He invented the tartan look for Punks and he and Troy started producing tartan bondage trousers – the height of Punk fashion, buying the material cheap in Petticoat Lane or Brick Lane, carrying the bales of cloth back on the bus, and getting an elderly Jamaican in Battersea to make it up. Often George arrived late for work loaded down with old clothes which he had bought cheaply in a local junk shop. He and Troy celebrated their newly-acquired treasure in the next door wine bar, Bouzy Rouge, one of the few Chelsea hostelries prepared to serve Punks.

George and Jane were close friends by now, "always giggling together and telling each other off", says Troy. When George was not working he would often meet Jane at her bank and the pair of them would go window-shopping along the King's Road. Or else Jane would go round to George's house after work and listen to him singing along to Irish rebel songs on the record player. Since Jane and Lennie had started going out together, the three of them spent more and more time in one another's company. They formed a happy little trio until George went and spoilt it all by falling in love with Lennie.

While George, typically, wanted to be entirely open about their relationship, Lennie was determined to keep it quiet. Particularly from the girls, particularly from Jane. "Come on, Lennie, admit you're gay. Let everyone know," George teased him in front of everyone. And Lennie would shy away, saying: "Oh, leave me alone."

Relations between Jane and George became fraught. Terry remembers a party in Gravesend at which Lennie arrived with Jane and left with George – after a dramatic scene between George and Jane.

After another party in Gravesend George and Lennie disappeared together when they were meant to be sharing a cab home with Terry and a girlfriend. They were eventually found at the railway station, sitting in a little shelter right at the very end of the track. George and Lennie remained close friends for about a year, during which time they rowed frequently. "I've never seen such violent rows," recalls a friend of them both. "George was just so dramatic. George really did love Lennie and was very demanding of him because he loved him so much. He really did have a lot of feeling for Lennie.

"And Lennie was so desperately cagey about their relationship because although he was obviously homosexual he couldn't come out of his closet at all. He fell for George's charm, really. George's attitude was 'come on, let's do it. Let's fall in love'. Today Lennie refuses to discuss the relationship other than to say "George and I had a very special friendship. But it's up to George to talk about it – I'm not going to say anything to harm someone in his situation." He adds: "We were all fairly inhibited in those days but, then, we were all fairly young. George and I used to argue a lot but it brought us closer together."

Ironically, Lennie last saw George at the same place where they first met – the gay club, Heaven, which was then Global Village. "It was just after *Do You Really Want To Hurt Me?* was released," recalls Lennie. "George was surrounded by people asking him for his autograph. I told him I was really pleased for him and to keep in contact and let me know how things were going. He asked my address but I didn't have a pen so I told him to get in contact through my mum – but he never did. I expect he's just been so busy that he hasn't had the time."

Lennie knew George's parents quite well when they were friends and admits: "I don't think they liked me, really. I think it was because I was a bit older and they thought I was an influence on their son." He adds: "In fact, I wasn't. I think he was more of an influence on me."

George

Lennie

4 *Chameleon*

*A*t the age of fifteen, George discussed his sexuality with his father.

"He sat down with me one day and told me he wasn't sure whether he preferred boys or girls," Jerry O'Dowd told reporter John Blake. "At first I thought he was simply trying to shock me because that was the kind of boy he was. But then I could see he was really serious and it was troubling him badly. He said 'what shall I do? Shall I move out?' I was really angry and I said 'why the hell should you do that? As far as I am concerned you are my son and that is it'. I told him I didn't think I was perfect myself and anyway why was he so sure there was something different about himself? Why was he telling me this? He said 'there's someone I love very much and he's a boy'. So I told him 'that doesn't mean you are gay. I've had a very deep affection for other men but that didn't make me decide I was gay'. I said that there were a few men I have met who I would lay my life down for. I really loved them but I loved them in a different way to the way I love my wife, Dina. And I think George's attitude towards me changed completely from that day. I think that was the time he really got to know me and I think he was genuinely shocked by my reaction. He thought I'd be angry but I wasn't at all."

Certainly, this was a time when George was testing out his capacity to outrage and some of his closest friends from this period cannot remember him being anything other than gay. "From what he told me I think he might have slept with a girl – very unsuccessfully – when he was about fifteen," one of his oldest confidantes told me, "but that was it." Even at the age of eleven, his drama teacher, Mrs Cankett recognised his homosexual tendencies. "Having come from a theatrical background myself it was obvious to me that he was going to be gay or at least bisexual. He was quite overt about it and totally uninhibited."

At school George spent all his time with the girls – "the boys hated him because they thought he was weird," says Mrs Cankett – and most of his male friends since have been gay or bisexual.

George himself has always been cleverly non-committal about his sexual preferences. When asked if he is bisexual he quips: "If I want sex I have to buy it." And questioned about whether he sleeps with men he retorts: "I never sleep. I try to stay awake whoever I'm with."

Perhaps it is better for George's public image not to be too specific about his sex life. Yet, many of his friends consider that he is now a big enough star no longer to have to hide the fact that he is homosexual. Even some of his most devoted fans accept his gayness – albeit reluctantly.

Besides, George has always been able to send himself up. Once, at the 100 Club, passionately greeting an old friend, he grinned at her bemused fiancé and said: "Don't worry about me, dear, I'm gay!"

George's father is now reluctant to discuss any conversation he has had about George's sexuality but he is happy to admit that he does not find it at all offensive. "If George is gay it's a genetic fact," says Jerry O'Dowd. "Gay people don't offend me. I think there's room for all sorts of people in this world.

"We're a very very close family and we've no hang-ups about that sort of thing.

"I remember hearing that they didn't accept gays in the services, yet when I was in the army there was a high percentage of batmen who were gay and the truth of the matter is that the services used them to do the best job that they could like clean the bloody officers' boots.

"The majority of gays are very decent people with morals the same as everybody else. They don't go around jumping on people which is the sort of narrow-minded concept our narrow-minded society has of them.

"I know a lot of George's friends who are way-out characters who set me back on my heels when I first met them but when I got to know them I found they were very nice people.

"I find George a very moral type of person anyway."

Certainly, George does not now believe in casual sex although he has admitted that, as a teenager, he did have his fair share of one-night stands. "When you're young, you sleep around and have this stupid attitude that you must get what you want while you can and when I was young my sex drive was quite high.

"But, when you grow up, you start to

George with girl   **George with boy**

Changing faces

realise that there's more to people than just having sex with them. I think sex and love are very similar things. They go together. I don't think I could sleep with anyone now unless I loved them. I think the feeling you have from having sex with someone you love is far more exciting than having sex with somebody you don't know."

And despite his endearing remark that he would rather have a cup of tea and a good conversation, sex *is* important to him. "Sex is something that everyone has to do and wants to do. It is much more important than art. Nobody is celibate. I don't think there is anybody who doesn't enjoy sex. It's a human thing, just like eating." And he is the first to insist that "love in any form is good. To be in love with a man or a woman is good. If you really love them it's not disgusting. I've never done anything I've been ashamed of."

In love, George is very affectionate, very loyal and very vulnerable. He falls hopelessly in love and is very demanding in return. Inevitably he has been deeply hurt over the years.

He has always been attracted to masculine men – "he doesn't like poofy people at all," says a close friend – who are mainly older than him, and those who know him best believe there have been no more than three or four long-standing sexual relationships in his life – none of which he ended himself.

"George has always been so desperately insecure that if he gets someone – even though he can see their bad points – his attitude is very much that he won't give up on a good thing," says a friend.

And George admits: "I am always grateful that anyone should want to go out with me in the first place. I've never ended a relationship in my life. Everyone I've ever loved I'll love till I die. So to call me a decadent person. . . how could anyone hate me?"

How indeed? Maybe only prudes and puritans do so – such as the Mormon Church who banned Culture Club's records from Brigham Young University in Utah; and the celebrated Australian prist, Father Frederick Nile, who ritually tore up photographs of George in front of his congregation, denouncing him as an "evil and unhealthy influence" for dressing up as a woman and making people confused about their sex lives.

Yet George is not a transvestite in the accepted sense of the word. "He is just a man who likes to emphasize that he is pretty," says a spokesman for the Beaumont Society, a support group for heterosexual transvestites. "Genuine transvestites are men who want to dress and behave as women without appearing in any way exceptional."

Nor, George insists, is he a drag queen. "There are hundreds of pubs all over England where there are drag queens you can go and laugh at," says George. "I'm not a drag queen. I've never wanted to look like Danny la Rue. I'm very serious. And I think if you want to confront the world with eccentricity you have got to have a good explanation. It's O.K. to be a clown in a circus but not to be a clown in a supermarket. I'm trying to make people more tolerant towards things that aren't harmful."

Many people would disagree with him and consider his justification rather too slick. But then, George has always been able to conjure up the instant logic to suit any occasion, as his family, friends and former schoolteachers know only too well. His detractors argue that Boy George is making homosexuality and transvestism fashionable and acceptable – particularly since he has a talent for producing such "logical" arguments to support them. His matter-of-fact approach makes the most outlandish behaviour sound normal to an impressionable audience. And George's audiences *are* impressionable. "I enjoy people not knowing what I am," says George. "I like the idea of 'ha, ha, is it a bird or is it a plane. . . ?'"

The remark is one of a stock of glib one-liners which he trots out at suitable opportunities. "Most people would rather sleep with a teddy bear than an action man," is one of his favourites. Another is "sex is just like eating a bag of crisps – quite nice but nothing marvellous". They are aimed at avoiding the issue and at side-tracking the interviewer, an art he perfected as a child. "I don't care what they ask me," he says. "I'll always have an answer for them." He recently told the American magazine Rolling Stone: "It doesn't really matter what I say about my sex life because everybody's got an assumption about what I do, although nobody will ever really know because I won't tell anyone. My sex life is very important and very private to me. I enjoy having sex.

"People say Boy George isn't sexy. Of course, I'm sexy. I'm just not sexy in the way David Lee Roth is. I'm not Tarzan beating my chest. I'm a different kind of sexy, far more interesting, I think."

What must be remembered is that George actually enjoys keeping the public in suspense about his sexuality. It is good for business and it is good for a laugh. And

George has a wicked sense of humour. "I wouldn't want to explain what I am to anyone," he says. "It would take the whole fun out of being me. Most people don't want to hear explanations – they're not interested."

And, after all, the whole fun of dressing up is to present a chameleon-like camouflage to the world. "You can't judge a book by the cover," says George, and he disguises his sexuality in the same way as he disguises himself. It is all part of the highly professional non-sexual package he has deliberately created based on the broad appeal of his personality. Yet he insists: "Boy George is not another character. Boy George is George O'Dowd."

Even so, the unavoidable mystique only adds to his fascination, as he is well aware. Much of George's appeal is his ability to fit into any situation and get on with anyone. He has always had the enviable talent of being able to emulate the lines of his father's favourite poem, If– by Rudyard Kipling, which go "If you can talk with crowds and keep your virtue,/Or walk with kings – nor lose the common touch. . ." Ironically perhaps, the final line reads ". . .you'll be a Man, my son!"

But, in his way, George *is* manly. "I'm not trying to kill some desire to be a woman," he insists. "I'm totally a man. And when I go into the bathroom in the morning I'm quite aware of what I am."

His capacity to love and be loved is enormous. And not just in a sexual way. Genuine affection is something George has craved since he was a small child. "I love cuddling with all my clothes on," he says. "Embracing is my favourite sexual position." And he told the television interviewer Terry Wogan: "I love everybody – anybody who wants to love me whether they're gay or straight or dogs, cats, budgies, any culture. . . I'll have anybody who wants me."

Like the chameleon, George has the natural gift of being all things to all people.

5 *"Just Good Friends"*

1977 and punk shock was in full roar. The mood was aggression, the sound – a cacophany of vehemence. Everyone wore black – presumably to match their thoughts. At the 100 Club and the Roxy, the punk bands spat out a dirge of defiance to an audience high on autism and amphetamines. Musical talent seemed to have become temporarily extinct. All you needed was a semi-articulate message of aggro and a name like The Damned, The Stranglers or Stinky Toys.

London's alternative night-life still spun around the gay clubs, and the Bexley contingent continued to spin with it. And in this hedonistic anything-goes environment George was meeting new people.

There was Philip Sallon, at twenty-seven one of the oldest of Louise's regulars and already the undisputed leader of outrage. While everyone else was looking punky, Philip followed his own style of flamboyance, wrapping himself mummy-like in bandages one night, wearing nothing but a few strips of strategically-placed gold lamé the next. There was Jeremy Healey, later to rename himself Jeremiah after George's father and become half of the notorious Haysi Fantayzee duo. And there was Marilyn, born Peter Robinson of Borehamwood in Hertfordshire, two years younger than George and, as yet, still a soul boy. The first time George met him he dismissed him as being a right little wally.

Even so, in the years ahead, George was to find in Philip and Marilyn, in particular, sparring partners able to compete, if not outpace him, in both their visual excesses and their sharp tongues.

George first saw Philip at a gay club called Bangs. George was wearing a ripped boiler suit held together with safety pins while Philip was dancing about in a long black skirt, black cardboard yoke, gold cummerbund, pit boots and leather gloves with horns on his head and with black lips. George was entranced and felt an immediate burst of affection for this outlandish individual who looked so totally different from anyone else on the scene.

Says Philip of that first meeting: "We just got chatting to each other. But I never got off with him! We're just good friends."

They met again at Louise's and this time Philip was sporting a top hat, suspenders, shorts and a jacket covered with Malteser wrappers. George was highly impressed. Philip already had a reputation as an innovator and a professional eccentric. "He

"Friends for eternity" – Philip and George

was genuinely outrageous," says Jane. "All of us did it for a reason whereas he just did it." Still the unchallenged leader of the London club scene, Philip's motivation really does seem to be a desire to make everybody happy, a contemporary Pied Piper as his father would have it. Today, George describes him as his closest friend, sharing many of his opinions, attitudes, and mannerisms, even the way he speaks. Philip also gave him the confidence to be himself no matter what the rest of the world thought. "Our friendship has nothing to do with sexuality," says George. "Philip is a friend for eternity. He's one of the nicest and most intelligent people I've ever met in my life."

These days, George can match both Philip and Marilyn when it comes to bitching and bossing although maturity – and success – have mellowed his tongue – in public, anyway. At the age of sixteen, however, he was still trying to assert himself among his elders, while defending himself against his antagonizers. "I was like a mirror for other people's insecurities," recalls George. "When I got on the train in the morning all I sensed was how uptight everybody was." He once swore at a woman who was laughing at him for wearing a kilt. "Why don't you keep your mouth shut?" he snapped. "Get your teeth fixed before you open your mouth!"

Admits George: "I knew it was cruel, but it was my only defence. I wasn't famous so I couldn't say – 'Listen, I've got loads of money, stuff it up your arse." He frequently utilized other people's faults as a form of verbal defense, shouting out "ugly" or "fatty" at anyone who scoffed at his own appearance. He also learned the art of the quick, bitchy one-liner as a means of expressing his anger. "I love you in that dress I never get tired of seeing you in it" is one of his favourites. In the end, he found he was not only able to cope with people laughing at him but it all went towards building up his own confidence.

Even so, his impetuous tongue frequently

came into conflict with his inherent need to be loved. "Whenever George had one of his outbursts of bitchiness he'd always be all sweet and apologise a few weeks later," one of his friends recalls. "The bitchiness was just part of the camp thing of being outrageous." And, to some of his fellow night-clubbers, at least, he was still regarded as "sweet, shy Georgie boy to be patted on the head."

By now the Roxy, previously a punky, men only, gay club called Shagarama's, had become as much of a regular haunt as Louise's. For fifty pence the fans could listen to the leading punk bands with up-and-coming groups like The Police supporting Chelsea or Cherry Vanilla. Based in Covent Garden's Neal Street, the Roxy was very much the seventies' answer to The Cavern, a cramped, grimy basement with condensation pouring off the walls. "It was," in the words of one of its devotees, "the pits". Lager was sold in cans and by the end of the evening the floor was thick with beer cans and fag-ends. Socializing was done in the toilets where the Ealing contingent started regular hairdressing sessions, providing an instant hack-and-peroxide for anyone outlandish enough to accept. In fact, so popular was this lavatory society that the management installed microphones and recorded the chatter to play in between the tracks of a Roxy live album.

And, then, there were the parties.

If there was one single feature that characterized this era it was the mobility of the young revellers. Distance was no object and, although few of them had cars, they would journey miles and miles for a brief visit to a particular club or party. Certainly, when George's old schoolfriend, Andy, and his twin sister, Laura, held a party at the beginning of 1977, hundreds of people poured in from all over south-east England, many of them arriving, fantastically attired, on the same train from Charing Cross.

Still fondly remembered by the guests as the party of the era and by the neighbours of this rather exclusive corner of Eltham Park as

58

the disaster of the decade, the riotous celebrations reached their crescendo with the arrival of some twenty police cars in the early hours of the morning. The party ended with Philip Sallon, dressed like a Roman emperor, mincing around the garden with two enormous police dogs snapping at his toga; the Ealing mob barricading themselves in upstairs declaring a legal squat; and George and Lennie hiding under a table in a locked unlit room after Lennie had pulled out the telephone wire to stop Laura's furious parents from calling the police. The grand finale consisted of dozens of policemen with dogs leading streams of multi-colour-haired people away in all directions. "It was," says Terry, "quite the best part of the evening."

There were also the regular bank holiday coach trips to Margate and Southend where everyone would parade around in their crazy outfits trying to avoid being beaten up by the Teds. Often they failed and Lennie started carrying a pair of ordinary jeans to change into when his bondage trousers attracted too much aggravation. Even George affected a compromise when the Ted aggression became too much for him by slicking his hair up into a quiff, pencilling on a moustache and wearing a studded jacket or drapes. By now he was going around with a punk friend called Michael Eggleton, managing between them to confuse both the Punks and the

Twins Laura and Andy

"George used to make out he was my lover" – Michael Eggleton

Teds. Another close punk friend of George's recalls: "Quite a few of us used to dress up as Teddy Boys in the end. We did it for a piss-take really – if you can't beat 'em, join 'em. We were all a crowd of screaming queens, so who wants to get beaten up by a load of big butch Teddy Boys who were motor mechanics and exhaust fitters? And, actually, it was quite fun because we always added a slightly outrageous element, anyway." Which is probably why, dressed as a Ted himself, George once got punched on the nose by one of the genuine articles.

Michael was a year older than George and a trainee for top fashion designer Jean Muir. George used to meet Michael at lunchtime at Jean Muir's Bond Street showroom and the two of them would share a sandwich and pose up and down Mayfair's bijou pedestrian thoroughfare, South Molton Street. In the evenings they did the gay clubs and the gigs – usually with Michael paying, and George often spent the night at Michael's parents' council flat on the South Lambeth Road. "He used to stay for weeks on end," says Michael. "He almost lived there. My parents used to think George slept on the floor but actually he shared my bed. We weren't lovers – good God, no – just good friends, although George used to make out he was my lover and hold my hand in the clubs. We used to talk about which men we fancied. George never really picked up guys in those days – he used to go for all the wrong ones, anyway, the ones who didn't like him, mostly weird-looking guys who weren't very jazzy or nice-looking. I go for jazzy guys with little legs, myself. Sometimes we'd accept lifts from blokes who fancied us – just to tease and get a car ride home.

"George and I were always looking for people to invite us to dinner. The first time we'd meet someone we'd say – 'oh, invite us round to dinner'. I was into dope but George wouldn't touch it. I used to invest my money in £5 worth of cannabis and that would last me a couple of weeks."

Even at that age, when many of his friends were experimenting with drugs of one kind or another, George had a strong enough mind of his own to refuse to go along with the herd. But, then, he had never done that in his life, anyway. He admits he did take speed along with almost everyone else, but that was primarily to keep awake all night and still be able to work the next day.

In Michael, George had the sort of playmate he had previously found mainly in girls like Tracy and Jane, playing with make-up, dressing up together and fooling around the shops. George and Michael often visited the millinary departments in the big Oxford Street stores like Debenhams and John Lewis to try on the merchandise and mince around in stilettos with handbags dangling on their arms. "People would look at us and laugh and call us silly names," says Michael. "Nobody minded us taking the piss."

In those days it was Michael who wore most of the make-up and George who often painted it on him. "I used to walk around like a clown but George would be scared to," says Michael. "We were always getting beaten up by Teddy Boys. We never fought back – they were too strong. I used to scream and sometimes I got away with it because they didn't know if I was a boy or a girl."

Back at Michael's parents' flat the two boys used to dress up in stilettos and skirts "with about four hundred petticoats underneath and dance around". Michael's father, a builder, did not approve of his eldest son's best friend. "George was rude to him and it really got my dad's back up," says Michael. "He answered the phone to him once and George said 'Is Michael there? . . . Well, can you get him?' My dad never forgot it."

It scarcely mattered because George was getting bored with London anyway. Now that his romance with Lennie was finished he was beginning to tire of the continual round of the same old clubs with the same old posers in them all. He felt the need of something different, a new scene with new faces and new ideas. Birmingham was the answer.

On one of his day trips to Southend he had met a wild dresser called Martin Degville, a charismatic shocker who worked as a chef in

Birmingham. Martin had issued George with an open invitation to come to stay and George decided that the time had come to take him up on it. His mother rang her younger sister Theresa, who lived in Birmingham, and asked her to keep an eye on him. Dina also made George promise to tell his aunt where he was living and to get in touch with her if he had any problems at all. "He was only sixteen," says Dina, "but an old sixteen. He was very mature for his age. In some ways he could have been eighteen or nineteen years old."

Led by innovative fashion designers Patti Bell and Jane Kahn, and Martin himself, Birmingham had a thriving youth scene of its own. In common with London it revolved around the outrageous dressers and the gay clubs but it was less cliquey and elitist and much more friendly.

George moved into the derelict rambling corner house at the top of Walsall's Goodall Street where the thrice-weekly market was

Painted loons – George and Martin Degville

held, and which Martin shared with Janet, Rhonda and Patrick, making sure to give the address to his Aunt Theresa. Janet worked for the post office, Rhonda and Patrick were unemployed. They paid around £5 each a week in rent and spent all the rest of their money on going out every evening and dressing up. It was a lifestyle that suited George perfectly.

Apart from anything else, it was the first time he had lived away from his home and he loved the feeling of total freedom. He had never even had a room of his own before, a luxury after a childhood shared with four brothers. Even the primitive living conditions did not bother him too much. With hot water only in the kitchen upstairs and the bathroom in the basement, it meant pumping the water into the bath through a long hose, and tearing up and down the stairs every couple of minutes to adjust the flow.

George was also impressed by the friendliness of the locals who welcomed him into their circle straight away. There was always room for another painted loon – and with Martin as his mentor that was exactly what George became. For the first time he began to wear make-up with a vengeance, painting his face blue or green, his neck red and dyeing his hair mauve. George compares himself and Martin at that time to the ugly sisters. "With him to compete with I just went over the top," he says.

Martin was just opening a clothes stall in Birmingham's Oasis market and, during the day, George helped him design and eventually sell the clothes, buying yards of material from the market and turning it into the kind of crazy garments they liked to wear themselves. Or he would hang out with the other kids at Jane and Patti's fashion and Victoriana shop, Khan and Bell.

In the evening they all dressed up and travelled the ten miles into central Birmingham by bus, meeting up in Hawkins, a thirties-style wine bar, or the Crown pub. Then on to one – or all – of the handful of gay clubs that catered for the likes of them. There was Barbarella's, a large barn of a place with three different rooms on three different levels. One played only reggae type black music while the largest of the three was where the bands appeared, anyone from Blondie to James Brown. The mood at Barbarella's changed as fast as the music. On rough nights there would be couples copulating behind the curtains. On smart nights it would be full of posers like themselves. Then there was Romulus, specializing in the rather more chic Bryan Ferry type look and the newest and wildest club of all, the Holy City Zoo.

George found the Birmingham scene smaller, cosier and more relaxed than London's. It was easier to move from club to club and if you happened to be with Jane or Patti you got into most of them for nothing, anyway. There was also more drinking and drug-taking than at home, neither of which greatly impressed George. Even at this young age he realised that being outrageous had to be done with style – which meant being totally in control. With stricter licensing laws than in the south the clubs shut promptly at 2am. Even so, the late bus back to Walsall could prove perilous for peacocks like George and Martin for the red-blooded Midlands working men did not take kindly to chaps wearing make-up. Once, a car full of drunks spotted them on the bus and followed them until they reached their stop. As the car screeched to a halt behind them and the men clambered out, George, Martin and Rhonda ran for their lives, ducking in and out of side streets, hearts hammering like anvils, until they could no longer hear the sound of their pursuers. Even indoors they were constantly threatened and harrassed by local heavies. Walsall was a notoriously tough working-class suburb. Gangs of kids would throw bricks and stones at their windows and tried to break into the house which stood alone at the top of the market place.

One day, help came from an unexpected quarter.

Market days were Tuesday, Friday and Saturday and then George and his friends would hang out of their windows and chat up the local cops. They befriended a few of them who would sometimes drop in for a cup of tea. On one such occasion, they were sitting talking to their new friend when a gang of louts started trying to break in downstairs.

"Leave this to me," said the policeman putting down his mug.

The youths outside were just about to put their boots through the front door when it was opened by a uniformed policeman.

"Can I help you?" enquired the cop pleasantly.

"Er. . we . . . er, we thought it was a club," stammered the would-be intruders weakly.

"Piss off!" growled the policeman. "These people are friends of mine. And if I catch you round here again. . ." He did not need to finish the sentence. The gang left meekly and never returned.

On Thursdays, everyone in the house collected their dole money and trooped down to Sainsbury's to buy a few basic essentials like bread, butter, coffee and milk. Mostly they dined at the local chip shop. Of them all, George was the most domestically-inclined. He had always helped his mother around the house and now he spent hours cleaning up the dilapidated kitchen, bitching at anyone who made it dirty again. He even invited his Aunt Theresa over to tea and introduced her to Martin and the rest of his new friends. Although outwardly a rebel, George could still not suppress his basic need for home and family. And, being George, he would not have wanted to anyway. He might disguise himself externally but he had never pretended to be anything other than what he was.

And, influenced by Martin, his appearance continued to grow more and more outrageous. When Michael Eggleton came up to stay for a weekend he was amazed at the change in his old friend. In London, it had been Michael who went over the top and George who egged him on. Now it was the other way round. George was prepared to go to any lengths to shock, and persuaded Michael to go out to the clubs with him wearing a man's suit and stiletto heels. The next morning George insisted they wear their stilettos down to the bakers to buy their breakfast. He and Michael walked right through the crowded market, their high heels clicking on the stone slabs. "The whole market stopped to look at us," recalls Michael, "and George absolutely loved it. So did I. Everyone was staring and nudging each other and it was just what he wanted."

George spent about a year in Birmingham. He then decided it was time to come home and brought with him both his burlesque look and several of his newly-acquired friends.

They arrived back in time to be part of a new era in the London night-club scene which was to influence George's life as much as he would influence it.

Michael Eggleton in party pose

6 *"One Small Dingy Hole"*

*B*illy's was a tacky soul club in the basement of 69 Dean Street in Soho orientated towards black tourists who occasionally managed to find their way down into its murky depths. When Steve Strange and Rusty Egan approached the owner offering to fill the club once a week with their friends he happily agreed to a trial run.

Until now, Steve Strange, born Stephen Harrington, had been a pale face in the colourful crowd. A shy nineteen-year-old from Gwent in Wales he had worked in a butcher's shop before following the punk scene to London where he hung around with the other fans. "An odd little chap" was the way that Peter York, social chronicler of the avant-garde scene, remembers him. Rusty Egan was the drummer with the punk band Rich Kids before he and his flat-mate Steve teamed up to change the painted face of London's sub-culture scene.

Like everyone else at Louise's, George was handed a black and white printed card announcing "BIG NIGHT AT BILLY'S. DJ RUSTY EGAN'S BOWIE NIGHT EVERY TUESDAY FROM 10.00 TO 3.30." Like everyone else he was there on that first night in September 1978.

The lukewarm over-priced cans of beer and working-man's club decor merely served to accentuate the extremes of what was to become a weekly extravaganza. Patterned carpets, vinyl-topped tables, gold velveteen upholstery and plastic padded walls acted as a bizarre backdrop to the exotica that was to pass before it. Here comes the bride . . . and it's Philip Sallon – in full-length white wedding gown and policeman's hat. There is Steve Strange, dressed up for the first time anyone can remember, as a dashing Russian cossack in white breeches and flowing shirt with pale blue cap, shoulder cloak and cummerbund and gleaming black riding boots. And Martin Degville, with his bright orange hair and red eyebrows, all dragged up in his best black and white kitsch Nazi uniform. And Marilyn, blonde hair backcombed and lacquered up into spikes, draped in what looks like a black spiders web. And George, whose evening wear ranged from a pink and blue tartan pyjama suit to the toy soldier look that was to evolve into the much-vaunted New Romantic style. And, above it all, Rusty Egan's sounds that really set these Tuesday evenings way out in a class of their own, loud electronic Bowie music and bands like Kraftwerk and the wild German punk singer Nina Hargen, the makings of disco as we know it now.

Photographer Derek Ridgers compares Tuesday night at Billy's to walking into a "Hieronymous Bosch painting – furtive but lively and with a dedication that's never been equalled since." And dedication was what it was all about. Now that punk had been popularised into high-street chic, its innovators craved for something new and exclusive to which to belong once again. Billy's was the answer and they were not about to relinquish it until they had polished and perfected it into nothing less than an art form. Compared to Louise's this was sophistication, with narcissism taking the place of sex. Any kind of sex. No one had time to fancy anyone else – they were all too busy adoring themselves. Besides, sexual encounters were impractical when so many people were held together with tacking stitches and safety pins. Pose and strut and even twitch to the synthesizers but whatever

you do don't damage your clothes – otherwise tonight's gala queen will turn into a pumpkin or, even worse, a boring old fart. "The trouble with all that lot down at Billy's," remembers one of the original Tuesday-nighters, "was that it was all 'darling, lovely to see you' while they'd be stabbing one another in the back. They were all friends but they hated each other as well. It was very shallow and you never really got close to anyone. You never really confided in them and you could never really quite trust them."

George, however, was in his element. Billy's was like a private fancy dress party with everyone seeking to outdo everyone else. "Oh, *dear!*" exclaimed George one evening, eyeing one of the Ealing girls up and down disdainfully, "nobody *ever* wears the same thing two weeks running." Yet, there were times when even he tired of the ultra-egotists and joined the Ealing schoolfriends, Selena, Nicola and Dij, just to relax, according to the girls, among a group who were "actually *enjoying* themselves and getting drunk, falling around and being *real* friends to one another".

Here you were judged entirely by what you wore and how you wore it. Not surprisingly, the young fashion students who were part of the scene were to recognise the commercial potential and start displaying their ideas on themselves. By the time Heroes' Night at Blitz was born the New Romantic look had arrived.

Blitz was an up-market wine bar in Covent Garden, favoured by the local music and graphic community. Five months after starting at Billy's, Steve and Rusty, searching for larger premises, moved their Tuesday night parties to Blitz. "It was there," says Steve Strange, "that everything gelled and blossomed. It became a meeting place for people with ideas."

Now Steve sat on the door deciding who would be allowed to enter depending entirely on what they were wearing, while Rusty spun the latest in electronic disco

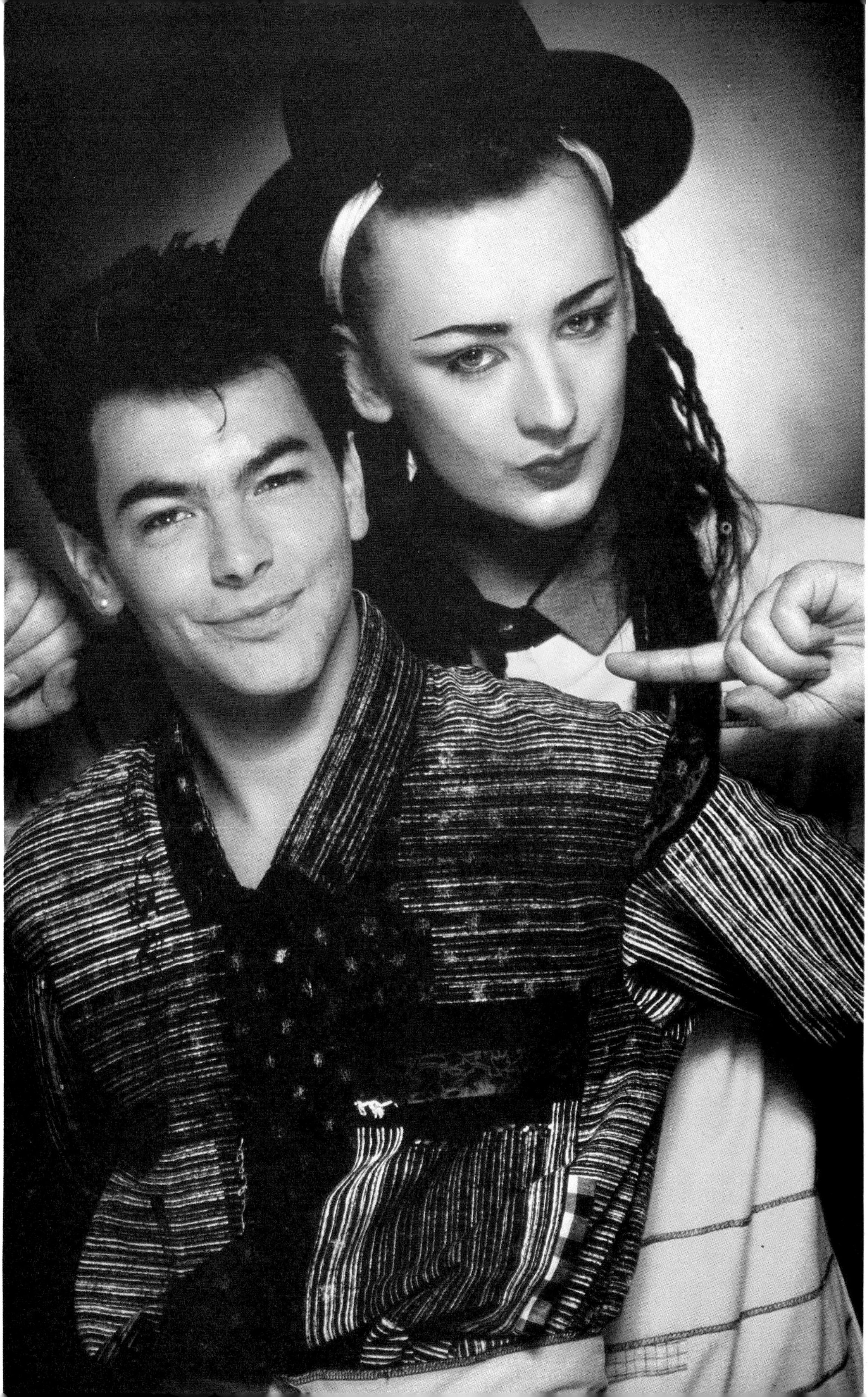

With drummer Jon Moss

A Cultural happening in Holland, 1983

Jon Moss

Marilyn

George

The cult before the Culture –
Blitz kids in 1980

George O'Dowd preparing for a coach trip to Margate, 1980

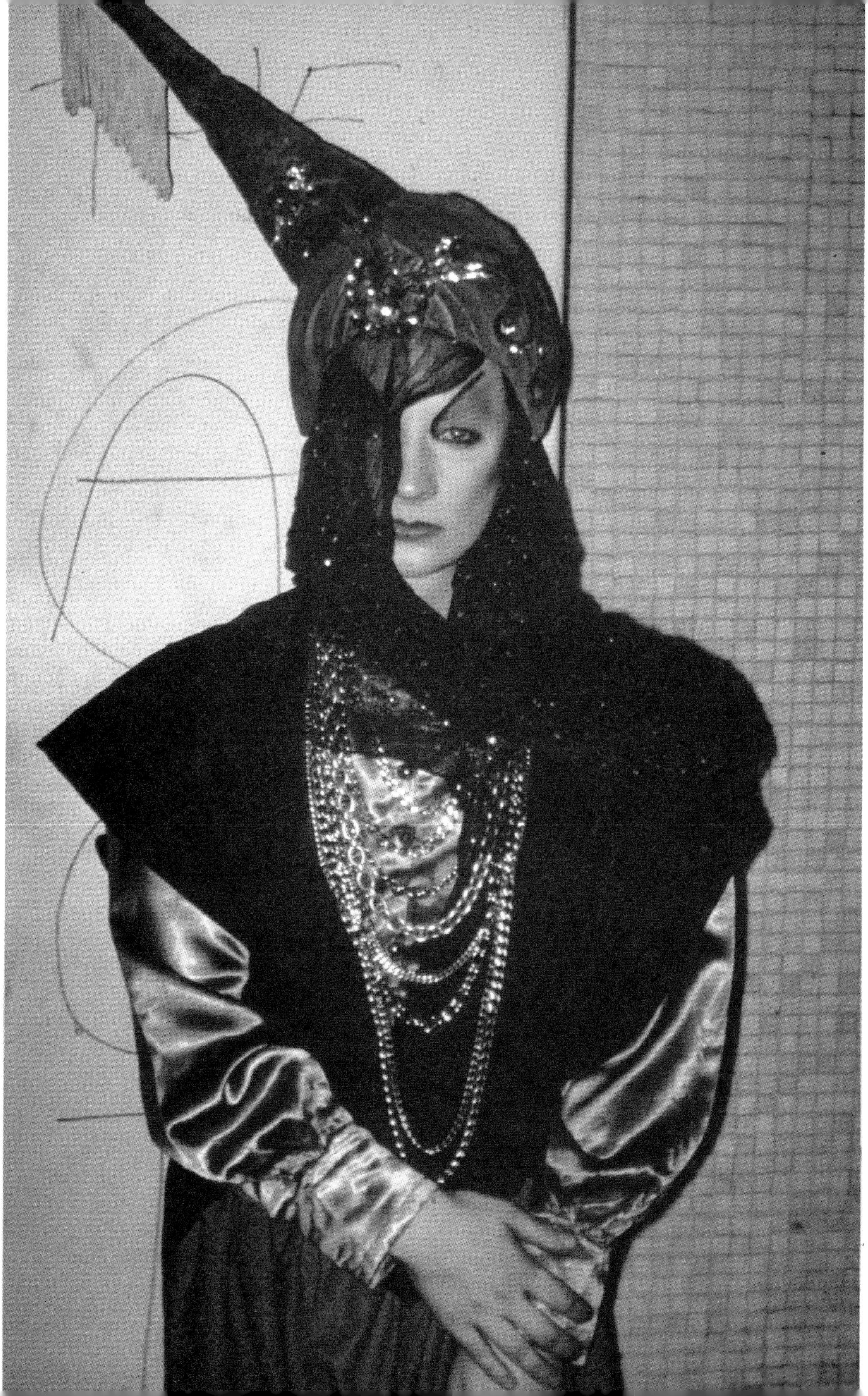

Glittering but not yet gold – Blitz 1980

Painted dolls – with Mike at Heathrow airport

On stage at London's Dominion Theatre, 1983

"All that creative talent . . ."

Steve Strange, the catalyst (centre), surrounded by (clockwise from the top) Jeremy Healey and Marilyn;
Martin Degville; George with Steve (in dark glasses); Philip Sallon

George and Selina – making friends

music and George worked as the hat-check boy. Fellow Blitz Kid, Bob Elms, remembers the flamboyant cloakroom attendant as having a liking for "theatrical slap, androgynous clothing and *grande dame* gestures". It was George's first official performing role in the scene he had helped to create – and he intended to make the most of it.

George's domestic life was coming together, too. After returning from Birmingham he had moved back with his family in Shooters Hill but his year away from them had given him a taste for freedom. Besides, now he was wearing heavy make-up he was getting more hassle at home and the journey up to town each evening was becoming a nightmare even for him. He now had a new friend called Andy Polaris who had grown up in a series of children's homes in Essex. At fourteen, Andy had started dressing up in plastic and pins and frequenting the local soul clubs. He, too, was in at the start of Billy's and, like George, was fed up with

risking his skin on the trains up to the West End. So, George started looking around for a suitable squat and found one in north London on a council estate just beside Kentish Town underground station. Towards the end of 1979, George moved in with Andy, Marilyn and a girl called Bridget whom George had rechristened Mad Myra because she looked like child murderess Myra Hindley.

The flat had a long corridor with a bathroom and a room each for Myra, Marilyn and Andy. Then there was another little corridor with a kitchen/living-room which was where George slept. The flat had hot water and central heating but no electricity, so it always smelt of paraffin lamps and the carpets were covered with black spots. Soot stains, however, were the least of their problems. Far more frightening were the local skinheads with whom Marilyn liked to flirt, winding them up to danger level.

The squat was on the middle landing of five levels above a courtyard, so that

Jeremy Healey and Andy Polaris "leading a life of Reilly"

Marilyn – "come on up, boys" – with Julia and George

everyone could see George and his flat-mates coming home in their frills and frippery. Marilyn was now right into his Monroe look complete with strapless black dresses, stuffed padded bras, crimped hair and stilettos. He looked stunning, the prettiest person on the scene where everyone else was contriving to look progressively more ugly. He had even perfected the screen goddess's mannerisms. "Hi, boys," he would purr down to the skinheads hovering in the courtyard below the flat. "Come on up, boys, come up stairs. . ." while the others tried to shut him up, only too aware of the likely consequences if the skinheads accepted his invitation and discovered he was a man.

Shortly before Christmas one of the gangs put a note through their letter-box which read *"You're going to get massacred by the Archway skinheads"*. The three boys all went away for Christmas leaving Myra alone in the flat. On Christmas Eve the skinheads turned up on the landing outside the front-door of

the squat. Myra, who was bald at the time apart from one little clump of hair at the back of her head, grabbed the carving knife and stormed out on the landing. "Do you want something?" she demanded, waving the knife threateningly. The skinheads took several steps backwards.

"I hope you weren't the ones who put that note through my door," snarled Myra. They turned and ran.

But while Myra excelled at strong-arm tactics, it was George who solved the problem of their lack of electricity. Ever practical, he found them an "annex" squat around the corner which still had electricity but no central heating. It meant that the four squatters could alternate between the two flats, using the original one when it was cold and the "annex" if the weather was warm. The latter, a ground floor council flat, was borded up which meant its inhabitants had to look outside the front door to discover whether it was day or night. Of the four of them only George and Andy were working,

George in a hat shop just down the road from Louise's and Andy as a messenger with a merchant bank. George hated the job but enjoyed trying on the hats. One day he went to work wearing a kilt – to the horror of the hat shop owner who happened to be wearing one herself. "You can't stay here in a kilt!" she told him.

"Why not?" asked George innocently. "If you can wear one, so can I. Besides, it looks better on me than it does on you."

This time the shop owner had the last word by firing him. "Losing the job didn't worry him much," recalls Michael Eggleton, "but he did miss the hats."

Steve Strange was also working in a fashion store during the day, a shop called PX in Covent Garden, which sold expensive High Tech leather gear to the Blitz clientele and others who were not but wanted to be. One evening Steve took George, Marilyn and Andy and a couple of girls for a drink at the notorious Coleherne pub in Earl's Court, haunt of the gay leather boys. Even George was startled by the heavy meat-market atmosphere with ageing queens on the look-out for rough trade. When they got home, George and Marilyn went back to the original squat while Andy decided to sleep in the one with electricity.

It was just before midnight when George, who was about to get into bed, heard a terrible banging that vibrated right through the flat. He peered out of the window and saw their next door neighbour brandishing a hammer and shrieking: "I'm gonna kill you! I'm gonna kill you!" as he battered his way through the flimsy wooden council door. George and Marilyn climbed through a back window and ran round the corner to the police station and then on to the other flat to wake up Andy. By the time they got back the police had arrived and were trying to control the hysterical man while everyone else on

Marilyn and George "laying the groundwork"

Lyn

the estate watched the proceedings with sleepy interest. Possibly it was the squatters' unconventional appearance that had pushed the man over the edge. He claimed it was their record-player playing too loudly that had driven him mad, unlikely since the flat had no electricity. . .

The police made the squatters move all their belongings out of the flat straight away so they simply carried them round the corner to their "annex" and settled down there for the night. But after a few more days in the dark, freezing flat with no water and the local skinheads trying to smash their way in, they decided to look for somewhere rather more salubrious. Besides, Kentish Town was really too far from Soho to suit their life-style. So George went out squat-hunting again and found just the place in Great Titchfield Street in London's West End. It was ideal – even without a kitchen. Far more important was the fact that it was five minutes walk from the clubs.

By now, Tuesday night at Blitz had become a sub-cultural institution. What the Blitz Kids wore today, the world wore tomorrow and the costumes ranged from Toy Soldier to High Tech to what the media dubbed New Romantic, the Beau Brummell regency-style look for men with flouncy ballgowns in taffeta, satin and tat for the girls. Surrounded by World War II posters, the ultra-elite paid £1 to enter another world. Anyone could come providing they dressed the part – any part, so long as it was totally outrageous. And, once inside, Rusty Egan's electronic synthesized disco music and the general atmosphere of a mannequin show, turned them all into robots. At Blitz there was never any chatting up or smooching or wild dancing or anything at all that was not superficial and contrived. Nobody wanted to get involved with anyone; nobody even wanted to be best friends. It was all about being perfect, faces immobile beneath tons of white panstick, never allowing a single emotion to slip past the flawless mask. The

conversation was limited to essentials: whom you had seen, where you had been and which parties to gatecrash tonight. Even so, friends remember George, still trying to assert himself in this rarefied atmosphere, bragging about the men he had slept with and how many at a time. Although style was now everything and sex far too messy and mundane to be a part of the scene, George was still trying to shock. And everyone, but everyone, was aspiring to be something – be it a writer, designer, musician, photographer, artist or hairdresser, all sharing a common faith that one day they would be *someone*. And that fact alone drew them like glittering magnets to one another, a positive conviction that this was the start of something dynamic and as long as they all stuck together they could take on the world. And win. "Failure wasn't any part of that scene," recalls one of the original Blitz Kids. "No matter what you were you knew you would be a success". And, in the meantime, you could dress up like a bishop or a biker and strike an attitude and become an instant star for the night.

The atmosphere of divisive exclusivity existed even within the club. Fashion designer Melissa Caplan remembers "there was a right and a wrong place to stand depending on whether you were an innovator or a copyist. And if you were an innovator you must never be seen with people who copied you. And we all ignored anyone we considered to be naff."

Along with "wally", "tourist", "hippy" and "boring old fart", "naff" was the ultimate in insults. And these superior young elitists – in common with so many other "in-sets" of previous generations – treated such people with the disdain they felt they deserved. "We used to be so rude and arrogant," says Melissa, "and terribly pretentious."

Certainly, the unwritten etiquette that existed at Blitz was daunting to anyone not at the pinnacle of that golden hierarchy. Basically, the innovators like George could

Melissa Caplan –
"rude and arrogant"

do anything and be forgiven, whereas the copyists had to abide by the rules created by the innovators which half the time only they knew anyway. The only other sure-fire way into that elusive inner sanctum was if you happened to know Steve Strange.

George had none of these problems. He had found his rightful position, way out in front of all the other posers and poseurs – both literally and metaphorically. As the cloakroom attendant no one could miss him. And, unlike Billy's which had been more like a private party, Blitz became a media event. Suddenly the world's press latched on to the fact that something was happening in London and on Tuesday nights at Blitz you could actually see it, feel it, photograph it, talk to it. Whatever *it* might be. They were there every week, firing flash bulbs and questions, utilizing these uninhibited show-offs to fill their pages and their airtime, to titillate the great uninitiated public. "When the press started coming," recalls Andy Polaris, "everyone knew that this was the meal ticket." And, feeling they were on the verge of a personal break-through, the Blitz Kids all co-operated. CBS wants to film a sequence in Blitz next Tuesday? No problem. Steve Strange would make sure that all the right people were present dressed to scandalize the American nation. The glossy magazines of Europe, always on the look-out for exotic sleaze, went overboard for this high camp scene where men dressed as women and women dressed as statues, and it was so fashionable to be gay that even if you weren't you pretended you were. They compared it to Germany before the second

world war, the ultimate debauchery before devastation. George, looking as if he had been plugged into an electric current, his long hair standing on end, eyes wide and staring through wild orange make-up, appeared on the cover of glossy magazines all over Europe. *Donna*, the international fashion magazine, used the photograph to illustrate their article on Eccentricity and Transvestism – "*from all over the world, nights full of madness and cheer*".

And, of course, George was a natural for all the media attention. Not only was he visually outrageous but he could talk. An instant quote on this? An instant opinion on that? George was . . . well, whatever. When the *Sunday Times Magazine* did a double-page spread of photographs on these "romantic rebels", it was George O'Dowd "one of several bejewelled incarnations" who appeared not once but twice. "*He wears Leichner greasepaint on his face and weird androgynous secondhand clothes*," declared the caption. "*His father is a builder: 'He worries that I'll get beaten up'*."

George O'Dowd with fashion designer Kim Bowen as they apppeared in The Sunday Times in April 1980

In fact, George's parents were totally bemused by the attention that their misfit of a son was receiving. "My father would call up and say 'Why are you in the newspaper?'" says George. "And I'd say 'I'm in the paper because I'm like a socialite.' He didn't understand. I didn't have a job, didn't have any money, and yet I was in the newspapers or magazines every week."

Today, George admits that his ambition in those days was "to be in every single newspaper in the country." It did not matter that it was for nothing more substantial than wearing make-up and dressing weird. He enjoyed being famous for doing nothing. For the first time he realised that he could have fun – and eat – without working and he decided to indulge in it to the full.

However, his close friend, Andy Polaris, now a singer with his own group, Animal Nightlife, believes it was rather more than that. "George knew what he was doing," he says. "We both did. It was a case of laying the groundwork, meeting the right people, getting yourself in a position where you'd have more chance than the average Joe Public to get what you wanted out of it. Going about it in a roundabout fashion it would take you ten years to get a record contract. After a while people were offering us contracts."

In those days, George's taste in music was typically catholic, revolving around soundtracks of musicals, T-Rex and old soul disco albums, all of which would influence his own eventual style. But he and Andy were too canny to grab at the first chance that was offered to them. "I knew George could sing because he was always singing around the house," says Andy. "And I knew he wanted to have a group. But he bided his time and waited until the climate was right."

Anyway, George realised there was still plenty of fun to be milked out of the status quo. "We were living the life of Reilly, really," admits Andy. "We were in the heart of London with no rent, no responsibilities, going out every night and enjoying ourselves." George seldom even had to pay to get into the clubs, being regarded as something of a tourist attraction, which was just as well since he was still notorious for never having any money.

Apart from the clubs there were still the parties. Gate-crashing was the big thing. And the grapevine ensured there were parties to be crashed every night of the week. Mostly it was Steve Strange or Philip Sallon who heard about them – or, occasionally, even got invited – and then they would go team-handed, travelling in convoy, meeting up either outside George and Marilyn's squat or Philip Sallon's parents' house in north London. Indeed, one of the simplest ways of becoming part of this elite little set was to own a car. Stewart Mechem had a Fiat 124 and was always in great demand on a Saturday night. He remembers "long snakes of cars" waiting outside Philip's home, filled with the kind of creatures seldom seen in suburban Dollis Hill. And all down the road, lace curtains would twitch as Philip's neighbours forsook their television sets to view even more outrageous characters playing out their personal fantasies on their very own doorsteps.

Then Philip would trip down his front path wearing his latest little number which owed nothing to anything except his own extravagant imagination, and the cars would rev up and roar off down the road as if in a gangster scene from a low-budget movie. George and Philip usually sat together, bitching and bantering with one another, with occasionally George bursting into a few bars of song, just to keep the troops happy.

"We would travel the depths of London and beyond, arrive at a party, stay there five minutes – by which time Philip would be bored – and then drive on to the next," recalls Stewart. "It was tremendous fun but we did spend a lot of time driving about."

Surprisingly, they never had any problem getting in. "We'd find out Debbie Harry was having a party, and we'd all go and freeload,"

New Romantics. Steve Strange with billionaire's daughter Francesca von Thyssen

remembers George, "just dress up and walk straight in. Confidence can get you anywhere."

"Philip and George would be at the front and it was like 'don't you know who *I* am? Get out of my way'," says Andy Polaris. "They were so arrogant that everyone thought someone must have invited them there. Besides – they looked so good that you could hardly turn them away. And once inside they were the life and soul of the party. Everyone wanted to know who they were."

Everyone. George was meeting the people who counted in the worlds he wanted to be counted in. "I wasn't interested in being part of the aristocracy. I wasn't the sort of person who went out of their way to be friendly with certain people. I wanted to be friendly with the sort of people I wanted to be friendly with and I wouldn't make concessions."

Whatever his motives, the doors were open and, if not George, everyone else was tumbling through as fast as they could. Steve Strange was the catalyst, the person who created the stage, the scene, the atmosphere that enabled it all to happen. But once you were on that stage it was up to you. And, although it was all ostensibly visual, there was more to it than that. "Creating your own look went further than your clothes," says Stewart Mechem. "It extended to your attitude, your outlook, how you talked, how you behaved. Everything. And it could go wrong because of such a tiny thing. Maybe you put a comb through the wrong part of your hair or maybe an eyebrow was too heavy. It had to be perfect. It was a tight-wire, and a tight-wire as sharp as the people you were mixing with. The reason that a lot of top fashion people have come out of it was because they knew how to walk that wire."

This striving for perfection, albeit, at this time, superficial perfection, was eventually to carry an extraordinary number of them to material success. It was a scene that attracted creative, ambitious people and once in it they fed one another with ideas and inspiration, forming the nucleus of an artistic freemasonry that was to sustain them on their way up and once they had got there.

Society hat-maker, Stephen Jones, has never forgotten the first night of Blitz when he was still a student. "I was knocked out by it," he says. "I really had a great time. I remember thinking 'my God, I do love this place. These people have something to offer'. Everyone was desperately struggling to be an individual. George was an individual. If you thought you were going to look at all like anybody else – you didn't wear it. It left us all with a sense of exuberance. And taught me to do it and not give a damn what anyone else thinks."

Melissa Caplan was also there that night. "We all thought we were the King or Queen or whatever. You tended to believe people when they said they would be something. Everyone knew what they wanted to be and if they didn't they knew they wanted to be something. You just didn't think about not doing things but about doing them. It was all about achieving success and doing what you wanted to do."

Says George: "I wanted so much to be successful I would have died for it."

When Steve Strange put on an unknown group called Spandau Ballet at the Blitz it set them on the path to fame. "Everyone wanted

"A shitty little club"

Blitz Kids. George with friend

to know who this band was," says Steve. "It got them that initial recognition." It all helped to contribute to Steve's reputation for being "exactly as far behind the avant-garde as the paying public was."

Today, the list of those original Blitz Kids reads like a 'Who's Who of the Best of British Talent'. Fashion designers like Melissa Caplan, Fiona Dealey, Stephen Linard, Stephen Jones; groups like Visage (Steve Strange), Blue Rondo (Chris Sullivan), Ultravox (Midge Ure); the current club scene is dominated by names such as Philip Sallon, Chris Sullivan, Steve Strange; and then there are the writers, photographers, artists, designers. . . the list is endless. And then, of course, there is George O'Dowd.

"It was incredible," says Steve Strange of those heady Blitz days of 1979-80, "all that creative talent coming from one small dingy hole.

"That's all it was – a shitty little club. Which was great."

7 *A Family Affair*

For George's eighteenth birthday on 14 June 1979 Philip Sallon threw a party for him at Planets, a basement club in Mayfair's fashionable Burlington Arcade. Philip was running a Thursday evening party night at the club, anyway, with George as the regular disc jockey. George invited his family and friends to the party, fairly normal procedure on such occasions, except that in George's case it was like mixing cement with icing-sugar to create a soufflé.

Few people would have attempted such a potentially combustible mix of people but George did not think twice about it. Unlike many of his friends he had never tried to compartmentalize his two lives. His family knew all about his "weirdo" friends and many of them had been home with him to Shooters Hill. On that first dramatic occasion when Philip met George's parents Philip noticed Dina O'Dowd's picture of the Pope, and squealed out: "Ooh – George, look who's on the wall!" George's mother cracked back: "Don't start or I'll get the Ayatollah and put him on the wall, too."

So, at least, George's family knew roughly what to expect. For George, whatever his faults – and he readily admits to being obnoxious, careless and selfish at times – is not two-faced. He may be a chameleon to the world, constantly changing the colour of his skin, but to those closest to him he has always been sincere. Indeed, this occasionally disconcerting honesty has been the cause of many of the problems he has encountered over the years: the fights with his parents and school-teachers, the rows

George with his mother – "he loved showing us off to everybody"

with his lovers, the fiery disagreements with his band. George has never tried to hide his flamboyance from anyone. For that reason, unlike David Bowie, he has never suffered the pressures of having to live with a separate stage persona.

So it was perfectly natural for George to mix his entirely normal family with his outrageously extraordinary friends without worrying that any of them would discover anything about him that they did not already know.

It resulted in a remarkable evening – and one which his mother sums up better than anyone.

"We were the only normal people there," remembers Dina O'Dowd. "They were all way-out dressers and, of course, we looked weird to them but they were the nicest crowd of people. They were lovely . . . smashing people.

"George was bringing us round to everybody and saying 'this is so-and-so, this is me mum and dad, that's me brother and that's his girlfriend. He loved showing us off to everybody.

"It wasn't our cup of tea but they were a nice crowd of kids. It's just a matter of people. Instead of looking at their clothes and thinking – tut, tut – talk to them. They want to do what they want to do.

"There was a lady, my age, who said to me 'aren't you really proud of him?' and I said 'well, yes' and she said 'there's not many eighteen-year-olds who would fetch their family to a club like this and be proud letting them speak to us. . .'"

8 Do You Really Want to Hurt Me?

Kirk Brandon

"George and Kirk were best buddies." So says Andy Polaris who was living in the Great Titchfield Street squat when Kirk Brandon came to stay with George.

In a house full of romantics, chimeras and freaks, Kirk was very much a boy boy. While the others lived out their fantasies beneath layers of Leichner, Kirk indulged his in leather jacket, 501 Levis and rockabilly boots. He was the James Dean of the eighties, the rebel with an only too predictable cause, the mean, moody hard man preaching a message of destruction, and a philosphy he sums up with the words "don't give a fuck for anything or anyone else around you".

It was an ideology so totally alien to George's own that it was perhaps inevitable that he should find it both intriguing and appealing. Besides, Kirk was five years older than he, and had a band of his own, and that put him streaks ahead of the rest of his friends who were still aspiring to be something other than aspiring.

A grammar school boy from Torbay in Devon, Kirk left school at fifteen and came to London a year later, working first in the meat market at Smithfield and then as a street salesman peddling cuddly toys, belts, handbags and umbrellas out of a suitcase. "I was a good umbrella salesman," he says wryly. He was with a group called The Pack before forming Theatre of Hate, a rough tough rock and roll and rebellion band which aimed to sell both records and revolution.

George's own revolution had always been entirely personal and he was fascinated by Kirk's vehement dogma. It had never occurred to George to try to *alter* society. He just wanted to stand out from it. How could you be different from everyone else if you forced them to become the same as you?

He went along to all Kirk's gigs with him, helping Kirk's manager to set up the equipment, even holding up the amplifiers himself to prevent them crashing down on to the gyrating audiences working themselves up into a frenzy of anarchy.

George was enormously proud of Kirk and, as always, when he fell for somebody, he made no secret about it. At one concert at the Music Machine in Camden Town where Theatre of Hate was supporting the punk band Department S, George, dressed as Boadicea, grabbed an old friend at the bar and pointed to Kirk on stage, saying – "Look, look – that's my new boyfriend singing!" And he covered the walls of his room in the squat with 'I love Kirk' and 'George 4 Kirk' graffiti.

For his part, Kirk admired George's nerve. "I thought he was a very brave bloke, as a matter of fact," says Kirk. "He used to go out in the street in the middle of the afternoon, dressed up as Britannia, and he didn't give a fuck. Which was great. It took a lot of bottle to walk out like that with everyone wanting to punch his face in. The majority would dress up like that to go to Blitz in a taxi cab or a friend's car but it was only the Georges and Marilyns who walked around on the streets looking like that and getting into the fights over it." He adds: "George is a genuine bloke. He's a hundred percent. You can't fault him. He's a bit bitchy – sure; he shoots his mouth off – so what? But the ratio of sense he talks to rubbish is about ninety percent to

ten. Georgie does tell the truth."

Kirk also approved of the fact that, like him, George "didn't give a fuck about money. He'd take it if it was there but he didn't care." In those days, the squatters lived by their wits, stealing when necessary, using their guile and their guts to survive. Even George admits to stealing. "I didn't do it to be clever," he says. "I had nothing and resented going back to my parents for money."

George and Kirk went to the clubs together with Kirk playing the pinball machines while George posed with his other friends. Kirk's Glaswegian manager, Terry Rasor, despised Steve Strange and the whole Blitz scene. But, surprisingly, he approved of George. "I thought he was a stupid git at first," says Terry, "but he has got an awful lot of balls. The first thing I actually liked about him was when he came with us to a concert in Brighton at a terrible place which was packed and quite violent. We were setting up the equipment when George said 'I've got to go to the toilet' and he just walked straight into the Ladies without even thinking about it. And I thought 'he's all right' because if I was like that, that's what I'd do. I wouldn't give a shit for anything or anyone.

THEATRE of HATE

ReVOLUtioN

"At least George is an individual. He's himself and there's no one else like him. He's been through something and he'll go some place and he'll make an awful lot of people stronger for knowing him."

Inevitably, considering the differences in their personalities, George and Kirk clashed constantly. "Kirk was a very difficult person to get along with and he and George used to fight a lot," recalls Andy Polaris. "Kirk was often moody and gloomy and George used to think it was his fault. He was always asking Kirk 'what's the matter with you? What's wrong with you?' Kirk was so intense. I don't know what it was that George saw in him. He was good-looking but there must have been something in him that he let on to George that he didn't let on to anyone else."

Another friend remembers a party at the squat one freezing winter's night in 1979 which ended around 5am with the music still blaring and George leaning out of a third-floor window, covered in purple make-up, screeching into the night "I love Kirk! I love Kirk!"

Today, Kirk admits to being still fond of George but denies that they had a sexual relationship. Even so, there is no doubt that George had a tremendous crush on Kirk. He even got on with Terry Rasor who called him "an old poof" and read George's lyrics for him. "I used to tell him they were good," says Terry. "They were. He's a good poet. It was obvious where he was going and what he was doing."

It was Kirk who gave George the final shove in the direction he wanted to go. "Georgie was always talking about how he'd like to sing and all that and in the end I said 'stop whingeing and get in a band,'" says Kirk. "So we put the band together and that's how it started."

Many of George's friends believe that he wrote the words of *Do You Really Want To Hurt Me?* about Kirk. George has always denied it, although he has admitted: "Everytime you get hurt in love you write a great love ballad.

"Love is such a time-consuming thing and it eats away at your brain and it gives you damage," says George. "I do and I don't like being in love – it's a kind of love/hate thing with me."

9 "The Best Party We'd Ever Had"

*A*fter about a year in the Great Titchfield Street squat, George and his friends moved around the corner to another one in an old Victorian terraced house in Carburton Street. Before they left they threw a demolition party. They invited everyone they knew to help them smash the house to pieces. Their plan nearly backfired when they found someone still living in their new squat when they took all their belongings around there in the afternoon, and had to bring them back again to Great Titchfield Street. They solved the problem by stacking everything they owned on the top floor of the house with someone standing guard over it and just hoped that their guests restricted their annihilation to the lower floors.

Before anyone arrived George got a can of paint and sprayed rude graffiti about the individual guests all over the walls. "It was really disgusting things about the people he knew were coming to the party," recalls Andy. "So when they turned up they were really annoyed." As intended, the two hundred or so guests took out their annoyance on the house and reduced the interior virtually to a pile of rubble. One guest remembers people poking the ceiling to make the plaster fall down. "There was no music, no lights, no drink – except what people brought with them," he recalls. "Just hundreds of bodies jammed shoulder to shoulder like sardines. It was so crowded

George and Marilyn at Breaking Glass party
"terrified of being chucked out like freeloaders"

that half the guests didn't even know when the police raided it." Says Andy: "The house was just smashed to pieces. All the bannisters went. Everything. It was like a real anarchists' party. The police turned up later and there were streams of police vans all down the street. It was great. The best party we'd ever had."

They moved into the new squat the following day with Andy installing himself on the top floor "because I thought people probably wouldn't be able to throw stones that high" and George on the ground floor "because that was where the electricity was". Everyone else received their electricity from a series of highly dangerous cables which the squatters connected up themselves. Marilyn took charge of it, pulling the plug whenever he had a tantrum and plunging the whole house into darkness. The rooms were large and bright and kept comparatively clean by their occupants but the stairs and corridors were always filthy. George filled his room with colourful clutter, dangling his hats, jewellery and hairpieces all over the walls on nails among the snapshots of himself with Lennie, Terry and Jane just as he had done in his bedroom at home.

Stephen Linard outside the Carburton Street squat

Also sharing the house was Miss Binnie, a self-styled neo-naturist, who used to sprawl naked on her bed to the delight of the occupants of the council flats opposite. George and the other squatters went to watch her and her three accomplices do a gig in Brixton which involved a complicated series of exercises done on stage to music with the intrepid neo-naturists waving a stick with a roast chicken on the end of it, with nothing between them and the audience but a colourful layer of body paint. Their act nearly brought the place down. There was also Paranoid Pete, a tough rockabilly photographer, who had an effective way with a hammer when it came to scaring off the local kids.

There was no bathroom in the house so the squatters took a weekly soak at the Oasis Baths in High Holborn and for proper toilet facilities sneaked into the hotel next door. And in the summer George and the other boys would go skinny dipping at midnight in the Regent's Park lake.

George's squat was one of several in the area but he was most friendly with the occupants of the one round the corner at 65 Warren Street. There lived George's old friend, Jeremy, from Haysi Fantayzee, along with a crowd of young fashion and art students including Melissa Caplan, Kim Bowen, Stephen Linard, David Holah and John Maybury. Stephen Jones had his workshop there and remembers: "We were all slightly more elitist than George and Marilyn because we'd all been to college and had great intellectual conversations and they just, basically, came from the suburbs and dressed up, we thought, a bit too much."

Indeed, while George and Marilyn believed in accentuating the positive perhaps a little too crudely for their neighbours, the Warren Street students were considerably more lofty in their pretentions. "Most important was the unobvious," recalls Stephen Jones. "Edith Sitwell's photograph was in everybody's room. Grandeur, formality, hauteur – that was what people were after; a certain polished perfection and a certain quietness."

George had no time for such subtleties. He was much too busy posing for the photographers, who flocked around their front door, and proffering instant opinions on anything and everything. Marilyn, however, spent most of the day in bed, rising only at dusk to slip into his alter ego and flutter off around the clubs.

"Nobody took it seriously," says John Maybury of their squatting days. "It was all about having fun in a sordid, miserable building that was falling apart."

And fun it was, sharing the discomforts along with their clothes and make-up, living entirely for the moment in an exclusive little world, mini-celebrities with nothing to worry about except, occasionally, the next meal. Usually, that was breakfast, often the only meal of the day, taken at the Casabella or Black Sam's, the local greasy-spoons, where big platefuls of bacon, eggs, chips and toast, drowned with endless cups of tea and cans of Coke, would cost about £1. The Italians who ran the Casabella cooked them all a turkey at Christmas which they took to a friend's flat in Fulham and ate in style.

In the evenings, George – always the last to be ready – would meet up with the other squatters at their local pub, The Northumberland Arms, where their camp exhibitionism greatly amused the barman. Even the elderly regulars from the council estate got used to them ". . .ever such nice kids really", they would mutter to one another watching the free floor show put on by George and his friends.

When the kids from the council estate grew troublesome, hurling bricks through their windows, and stones and abuse at the squatters when they walked down the street, it was George who sorted them out, giving them a verbal lashing that sent them scurrying for shelter. In fact, the kids quickly accepted their eccentric neighbours when

reporters and photographers began hanging around the area. "They'd never seen anything like it in their lives," says Andy. George even won over the children's parents with his Reader's Digest repartee and the mums started inviting him round for tea to give him clothes and "treat him like the Queen Mother".

The squatters continued to gate-crash parties, frequently getting their photographs in the tabloids, outrageously dressed at some party to which they had not even been invited. Writer David Thomas recalls the night George and Marilyn swanned off to the opening of Hazel O'Connor's film *Breaking Glass*. "The doorman let them in like stars but once inside they were terrified of being chucked out again like freeloaders and spent most of the party in the Gents, emerging just in time for the obligatory photograph." At a Spandau Ballet concert George charged the photographers fifty pence a pose. He was regularly seen on *Top of the Pops*, prancing around in the background with the other starstruck kids. And, dressed as Boadicea with a winged helmet made by Stephen Jones, a Union Jack shield, a fork and white stilettos, he even took the good-humoured plaudits of the crowd outside Buckingham Palace during the Trooping of the Colour.

In the words of David Thomas, George was one of a group of hard-core trendsetters prepared to "dress up like any kind of wally if it meant a couple of inches of newsprint". Says George: "I was always interested in celebrities and I was desperate to become one myself".

Now he was changing his look every week, growing ever more theatrical and daring, dressing up in anything from a nun's habit complete with crucifix to a Japanese kimono, disguising himself as an Arabian prince one night and Carmen Miranda, Marlene Dietrich or Mary Magdalen the next. And always with the appropriate, skilfully applied make-up.

"During the club scene I wanted to look more outrageous than anybody else because

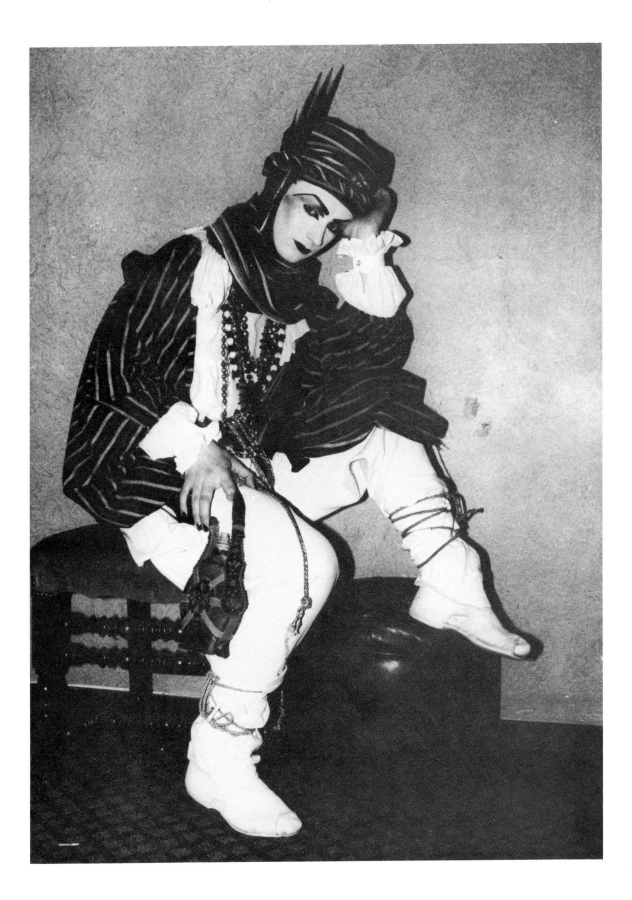

George – "I wanted to look pretty without looking grotesque"

George with dress designer Michele Clapton – "grandeur, formality, hauteur"

Andy Polaris – "the press were the meal-ticket"

Jeremy Healey – pre Haysi Fantayzee

Stephen Jones – "a certain polished perfection"

George with Stephen Linard – degrees of elitism

A feather in Steve Strange's cap

I thought most people looked really awful," George now admits. "Also, I wanted to do it properly. I didn't want to go out with make-up on and look like an idiot – which a lot of them do. I wanted to look classy, and pretty without looking grotesque.

"A lot of people said to me 'you look ridiculous but your make-up's done well'. I can cope with that kind of insult."

The Peter Benison model agency signed him up to represent their "new, weirdo side" and George featured in an advertisement for the Trustee Savings Bank and a commercial for British Airways. The latter, in which George is seen walking into the London nightclub Stringfellows, while a British Airways plane flies overhead, was shown on television on the day of the Royal Wedding. "My mum was really pleased," recalls George.

And when the Daily Mirror wanted someone to model for a fashion article about the crazy new London fashions, their caricaturist, Ralph Sallon, naturally recommended his son's friend. The resulting full-length photograph of George on the woman's page was captioned "*Flamboyant: George O'Dowd, 19, wears Chinese slippers (£3.99), old school trousers he tapered himself and leg warmers. A black crêpe Twenties dress – 20p from Oxfam – is pinned round his waist. Various tassel belts were picked up for a few pence, as were the long scarf and Oxfam beads around his neck. He got the wooden cross from a friend, the crimplene blouse from his mum. A black felt hat and assorted earrings round off the outfit.*" George was getting the mass attention he craved. But, it was not enough.

Now he wanted to prove that he was more than just a pretty face. "I'd made myself into a minor celebrity but I realised that a lot of people were inviting me to parties purely because I looked outrageous and I'd go along to parties where there were a lot of pop stars and I didn't fit in. I just didn't fit in with them. So I just wanted to do something that

George and Julia – playing statues

Andy Polaris – playing it cool

Girlish giggles

Arresting bride meets jail bird

I thought was more valuable and that's when I really became involved in music."

At last his single-minded yearning for success had found an outlet. "Being logical I'd set certain goals for myself but I also kind of fell into things by accident – like music," says George. "No matter what anyone thinks it isn't something I had planned." It was, however, the most likely target for his talents. Now all he needed was the vehicle.

It came along driven by that contemporary manipulator of the music and fashion scene, creator of the Sex Pistols, Malcolm McLaren.

McLaren had taken over Adam and the Ants and, having fixed them up with a new pirate image, he whisked away the Ants to form a splinter group of their own called Bow Wow Wow. All he needed now was a lead singer and he found her working Saturdays at his local dry cleaners, a fourteen-year-old half-Burmese girl called Annabella Lwin. Still dissatisfied with the end-result, McLaren looked around for someone else to enhance his new commercial package.

The first George knew about it was when he heard that McLaren was holding an audition at the Rainbow Theatre in Finsbury Park to try out hopefuls singing jazz songs. George already knew Matthew Ashman, Bow Wow Wow's guitarist, and Matthew encouraged him to have a go. The audition was not a success but George bumped into Malcolm McLaren at Planets a few evenings later. "I was really drunk," recalls George. "I went up to him in stilettos and a big straw hat with birds on and said 'I really want to sing with Bow Wow Wow and he just *looked*!" The approach worked, however, and George got invited to do several gigs with the group as Annabella's co-vocalist, Lieutenant Lush. They included one at the Rainbow where George sang the encore instead of Annabella and received an outstanding ovation and the following verbose review from the *New Musical Express*: "*Rumoured to be the new singer, a person called George guested on one rockabilly song amidst a whole pile of*

George's "viperish flamboyance" impressed one reviewer of Bow Wow Wow

old-fashioned encores. George's viperish flamboyance immediately shifted the sexual implications and radically altered visual tension; it was a different group. Annabella is openly unskilled: George is kind of glib. Both possess an amateurism that rubs attractively against the Wow boys' professionalism."

At the time, George was pleased and flattered to be invited to join the group but in retrospect he believes that McLaren only asked him in order to buck up Annabella's own performance. "Basically, they got me in because I wore a lot of make-up and looked a bit effeminate," he later said. "It was just to frighten Annabella, insult her femininity because she wasn't shaking her tits or lifting her skirt like Malcolm wanted her to. He got furious with her because she was always going on about being an air hostess. In the end, though, she got better and better and they didn't exactly throw me out. I just went round to see Malcolm and he hid behind the curtains!"

And McLaren himself admits that he put George in the group "because Annabella was too much of a problem. She was a good idea and that's terrible. . . George was a person, he had a thing of his own."

Even so, his three months' stint with Bow Wow Wow gave George some experience of singing professionally on stage and got his name in print for being something other than a freak. Asked whether George had joined Bow Wow Wow permanently McLaren told the music press: "George isn't part of the band but he should have a band of his own". Today, George is insistent that McLaren had nothing whatsoever to do with the fact that he eventually formed his own group. He believes it was Matthew Ashman's influence that got him in Bow Wow Wow and is adamant that he is not one of McLaren's protégés. Nonetheless, George was slowly edging his way towards his ultimate goal.

In the meantime, he fell into something else by accident – namely the fashion business. His friend, Mad Jeannie, heard that the Royal Shakespeare Company was looking for a stylist to produce an "authentic punk look" for its new production, *Naked Robots*, and recommended George for the job. George went in search of costumes and found just what he needed at a clothes shop off Carnaby Street called Street Theatre. He persuaded the owner, Peter Small, to lend him the outfits for nothing, in exchange for a mention in the RSC programme. "I used to be so rough with the actors," says George now. "Like a footballer. And I made all the women look like drag queens. They hated it but I like drag queens."

Peter Small was more impressed with George's approach and offered him a job helping out in Street Theatre and his other shop, the Regal, when the RSC job came to an end.

By now the fashion industry, spearheaded by many of the Blitz Kids themselves, was sitting up and taking notice of what was happening in the clubs. Shops, boutiques and stalls were sprouting everywhere with places like the Kensington Market undergoing a resurgence of energy and inspiration.

Among the many ambitious youngsters contributing their ideas to the new movement was Sue Clowes, a twenty-three-year-old fabric designer who had started her own kitchen-table industry using her prints on T-shirts, cushion covers and scarves. Peter Small discovered her selling her designs in the Kensington Market and gave her £50 to teach herself how to cut patterns and then employed her to produce designs and patterns for Street Theatre. When he opened another shop around the corner called The Foundry, he asked Sue to design a series of experimental clothes with print, and George to run the shop and sell them.

Now George had the chance to put to use the various facets of his personality, testing his abilities to see how far they would stretch. Peter says that he employed George

because of his "personality and the fact that he was good at things like display and had an eye for settings. He was also an excellent salesman. He had a flair for knowing how clothes should look. If somebody tried on a dress he'd do something to it or add an accessory to make them look good in it."

At the Foundry, George helped to create some of the fashions "working with Sue to produce a range of printed T-shirts and printed dresses which he used to wear himself".

These were the famous outfits that were to launch Culture Club, the red, black and yellow designs depicting religious imagery,

Sue Clowes and George outside the Foundry

Bombers, roses and religion make up Sue Clowes' famous design

bombers and roses, and over which George and Sue eventually fell out.

The relationship with George grew even worse when a newspaper misquoted Sue saying that George had "short fat hairy arms and a fat arse."

"George never believed that. What I actually said was that because he's a larger-than-life character I made the sleeves bigger, the bottom bigger and the legs bigger when I was designing for him," says Sue.

Either way, she never worked with him again although those original Foundry designs are part of pop music history.

By now, Camden Council had had enough of the squatters in and around Warren Street and tried to evict them in order, they said, to turn the site into a car park. George, ever the spokesman for the group, went to Marylebone Court to contest the action, modestly dressed for the occasion in his black bondage outfit. But his articulate discourse on how the squatters had improved the properties did not impress the council officials. It was one of the few arguments George has lost.

The squatters were forced to split up. Stephen Jones succeeded in getting four council flats simultaneously "a world record!" to rehouse a dozen of them; Andy went to share a house in Brixton "the first time I'd ever paid rent and the most awful place I'd ever lived in"; Marilyn moved to Los Angeles for a year where he got heavily involved in the drug scene – "I wanted to try everything once and I did"; and George moved into a rented flat in nearby Goodge Street with Mad Jeannie.

The party was over.

10 *Band of Hope*

George

Jon

Mikey

Roy

*A*mong the Rainbow audience watching George indulge in his "viperish flamboyance" with Bow Wow Wow was a young junior Artiste and Repertoire man for EMI records. Ashley Goodall had seen George around the clubs "with everyone going round talking to him almost like he was the star attraction" and had often wondered whether he could sing. At the Rainbow he heard him do *Cast Iron Arm* and was bowled over. "I thought 'crumbs – who *is* this guy?' He looked extraordinary, he sang brilliantly with a lot of guts, and he moved like a natural. There was no doubt about it: he was a star."

He tracked George down and asked him if he wanted to do a demo. "Yeah," said George, "I'm just getting a band together."

It began with Mikey Craig, the grammar school son of a Jamaican singer who was determined that his seven children would do something a little more sensible than just become musicians. He even refused to allow Mikey to take part in the trials for Fulham and Brentford Football Clubs when he was invited to do so. Work came first in the Craig household. Mikey disagreed. He discoed his way through his teens, first as a dancer, then as a DJ in a Soho club. When a friend lent him a bass guitar he jumped at the chance to make music himself, jamming with friends and playing with groups of hippy musicians. One day he saw a picture of George and Annabella in the *New Musical Express* with a story suggesting that Malcolm McLaren was thinking of forming a separate band with George. Mikey rang a friend who worked for McLaren and asked him to introduce him to George.

They met in Philip Sallon's club, Planets, where George was disc-jockeying, a pint of lager and blackcurrant by his side. "I sensed a lot of power around him, and strength," Mikey recalls. "Not physically, but just the aura he was giving off was positive and I liked that. He was playing *Sugar Sugar* by the Archers and all that real old nostalgic stuff."

Mikey told George he played bass and asked him if he wanted to form a band. Wondering how on earth he was going to start one with just a bass player George nonetheless decided he had nothing to lose. Besides, he liked the look of Mikey.

"OK," he said to Mikey. "Let's do it."

It was Kirk Brandon who put George in touch with Jon Moss. Jon, who was illegitimate, was the adopted son of a middle-class Jewish family. A promising young boxer who left his London public school with three A-levels, he started playing the drums when he was fourteen. He turned down the chance to read Greek at Cambridge University in favour of making his own way in the world which he failed to do with a variety of short-lived badly-paid jobs. He decided to concentrate on music and joined a succession of punk bands including The Clash and The Damned, achieving the dubious accolade of being voted "the prettiest punk" by a poll in a teenage girls' magazine. Now he was out of work and waiting for something to come up, when George rang.

They met in a rehearsal room in south-east London and took to one another immediately despite the fact that Jon hated posers and Blitz and everything to do with the dress-up-and-look-at-me scene. "I'd actually met George about six times before I realised I'd met him because every time he looked different," says Jon. "I went to a party once and thought he was that Siouxsie out of

Siouxsie and the Banshees. Another time he had his hair all up in the air and white and I thought he looked really disgusting and I didn't want anything to do with him then."

This time, however, George and Jon hit it off. "He was all made up, wearing outrageous clothes and I wasn't used to that sort of thing. I was struck by his amazing charisma and how friendly he was. He was very down-to-earth."

Says George: "When Jon walked in with his drum kit he said 'what do you want me to play?' And I said 'I don't know. Play something.' I didn't want a backing musician – I wanted him to join the band and make it what it is." That suited Jon perfectly. George invited him to do a number with himself, Mikey and a guitarist named John Suede. They did a song called *Mask* which impressed Jon not at all but as soon as he heard George singing he changed his mind.

Roy Hay replaced John Suede as the group's guitarist. An Essex docker's son, Roy got his first guitar when he was fifteen, having learned the piano since he was a small boy. He was working as a hairdresser when George asked one of Roy's friends, a regular customer at Street Theatre, whether he knew a good guitarist.

Like Jon, Roy was impressed with George's voice. It was the first time Roy had met someone who could actually sing and he was excited. George was, too. He liked Roy's playing and the fact that he came from the suburbs rather than the club scene. Roy had already played with a band at home and was ambitious to make it to the top. That fitted in with George's idea of building "a musical force" rather than employing three uninspired musicians to stand behind him. Aware of the importance of his own family background he wanted to recreate that feeling within the band.

It was Jon who took over as the brains of the band. "If we were a proper organisation

I'd be the public relations officer and Jon would be the bank manager," says George. "Jon looks at everything in a practical way. I'm the opposite – I look at everything emotionally." It was Jon who insisted they change their name from Sex Gang Children and Jon who suggested a new approach. After years of playing in punk bands, Jon was determined that this one would be commercial. He was tired of being part of a cult minority. Now he wanted to sell records.

They chose the name Culture Club because George wanted something that sounded "global" without being too pretentious. Initially, they dreamed up Caravan Club but it did not sound quite right. Culture Club was better.

Ashley Goodall had stayed in touch with George but he failed to convince his bosses at EMI that here was a group worth signing up and, anyway, George was worried about whether the mighty record company would market them in the right way. He decided to

wait until they had polished themselves up before worrying about a recording contract. In the meantime, they needed a manager.

"When we started we wanted to make sure that the business side of the band was sewn up totally," says George. "At first Jon took very much a business attitude towards the band. He wanted to make sure that everybody didn't turn round in two years time and say 'God – what have we done?' He took over the business but then he decided it was becoming too much for him. It was interfering with his musical ability."

George, with his customary astuteness, realised how important it was to get exactly the right person to manage them. "I looked around at the other groups who had failed because they had managers who were very bad at business and just couldn't get it together," says George.

"If I get a sax player I don't get a friend, I get a sax player. If I get a backing vocalist, I don't get somebody I've known for a few weeks, I get a professional. You must have a positive attitude about what you're doing."

George's own positive attitude stemmed from having hung around other bands long enough to recognise their weaknesses.

"We wanted a manager who was not part of our scene and who would make sure we were still making money in five years time. So we looked around for a little fat bald man who was Jewish and we found Tony Gordon."

Tony Gordon had previously managed Lulu and Sham 69 and had the tough background of the traditional pop music manager, and the reputation for making record companies shudder. When George asked him to manage the band Tony did not even mention money. His first words to George were: "I think your music's terrible. You've got a good voice but the songs are terrible and too long, but I can see the potential. You could be great at what you're doing."

George was taken aback. "We know that," he told Tony. "You don't have to tell us. Are you interested?"

"OK," agreed Tony. But he refused to sign a contract suggesting, instead, that they "leave it in the air and see what we come up with for each other."

"It's very difficult when you go along and employ somebody on a business level." says George. "I feel a lot of affection for Tony. He's very Tin Pan Alley but he's also good at what he does, and that's what we wanted. "He did a lot of work for us that he never got paid for and that made us confident and made us trust him a little bit more."

In action at London's Dominion Theatre in the Spring of 1983 – "totally dedicated – a perfectionist"

11 *Virgin Birth*

*T*he letter on BBC notepaper was brief and succinct.

"Dear George,

Many thanks for taking the trouble to supply us with material on your band 'Culture Club'. However, after careful consideration it was our feeling that the group wouldn't be right for the program. Best of luck and much success for the future, and again thanks."

It was signed by David Croft, assistant producer of Riverside.

Today, David Croft shrugs ruefully, and admits: "I've had my leg pulled about it a lot. All I can say is that I used to listen to dozens of tapes and after a while your senses get blunted."

Even so, the note, written in the late spring of 1981, was by no means the first rejection that George had received. For months now he had been writing lyrics, making demo tapes and plugging away at producers to sell first himself and now the group. So far no one had been greatly impressed.

George was still working with Sue Clowes at Street Theatre during the day, developing the Foundry look that would become synonymous with Culture Club, while devoting every spare minute to practising with the boys. Peter Small and his partner Lizzy Joyce were among the first people to see the group performing live.

"George really held them together," recalls Lizzy. "It was his whole life. He was absolutely determined they would succeed, totally dedicated – a perfectionist."

For so long now George had been talking

about getting a band together that his friends had stopped listening. "Don't go on about it – *do* it!" was their typical reaction. Kirk Brandon was one of the few people who realised just how hard George was now doing it, spending every spare moment writing songs and practising with the band. For once, George was keeping a low profile.

Now he decided the time had come to show off his band to his friends. He booked an evening at a club called Foubert's, just off Carnaby Street, and invited everyone he knew to a mysterious 'Can't Wait Party'. About 200 of them turned up, exotically-plumed as ever, wondering what to expect. When they walked in, Culture Club was on stage, in full swing, with George, microphone in hand, behaving as if he had been at it all his life.

The general reaction among his guests was incredulity that George had finally got it together at last.

The band did a series of gigs around the country including one at the Holy City Zoo in Birmingham where George had spent many an hour posing in the past. A Virgin Records man saw them playing at Crocs in Rayleigh, Essex, Roy's home town, and invited them to do a demo tape. But, without any formal training to fall back on, George was still copying other singers from his record collection. The demo tape was not good enough to convince Virgin to sign them. Finally, George realised that there was only one person he ought to be sounding like and that was himself.

The initial teething problems were enormous. With no money and, apart from Jon, little experience, it was a case of learning about the business and each other as they went along. "None of us could do much at the start," admits George, "but it meant that we all evolved as a real band together."

And now that George had finally found a purpose he was determined not to waste a second. He still wrote all the lyrics and dreamed up the melodies but it was Roy who

helped to shape the music and Jon who had the skills to mould the songs into a commercial form. "George used to write songs just like long love poems but I taught him that there had to be a hook line repeated over and over again," says Jon.

"My songs were like art school poems," agrees George, "twenty paragraphs and pages and pages of words. Jon said 'where's the chorus? Where's the beginning? Where's the ending?'"

In fact, Jon had summed up George's inexperience the moment they met. "I saw that George was a very creative person who had no idea of organisation and that I could direct him towards success. He had lots of brilliant ideas with nowhere to go and he kept asking me for advice." It was the role that Jon wanted, anyway. "People tend to think that drummers are just idiots who sit behind the other members of the band and do what they are told. But I take over in a band. I start to manage it and shape it and I've got a very good instinct for hit records. George is very naive and the obvious hardly ever occurs to him, but once you point it out he learns very quickly."

Jon – "I take over in a band . . ."

George *was* learning quickly. He already knew a fair amount about the record industry from observing the other bands. He also had a keen instinct for what was right for him and Culture Club. He agreed with Jon and Tony who felt their arrangements needed a more professional touch and they recruited record producer, Steve Levine, whom they had first met through Ashley Goodall of EMI.

Their sound started to develop into something with a bit of character of its own. George decided that at last they were ready for a recording contract.

With the same astute single-mindedness with which he went after first a band and then a manager, George set about finding a record company that fitted in with his idea of what a record company should be. He wanted one big enough to have the clout and the marketing know-how, but small enough to provide the personal touch. Unlike most embryo pop groups who take what they are offered, George realised how crucial it was to have exactly the right kind of organisation behind Culture Club. Having got this far he was not going to leave a thing to chance.

The major companies were beginning to show interest in this promising new group with the highly marketable lead singer but George felt their attitudes were impersonal and mercenary. Even so, he agreed to do a series of demo tapes for them – providing the companies paid for the studio time.

By now Virgin, the young record company owned by public school entrepreneur Richard Branson, was back on the scene. They already handled artists like Genesis, Mike Oldfield and Scott Walker. George preferred their approach to the longer established major companies. "Although Virgin are as much of a bastard as anyone else they're very good at what they do and they are one of the few companies you can walk into without having an appointment."

That mattered to George who was anxious to extend the "family situation" he was deliberately creating within the band. After touring some of the big companies with Jon where everyone was closetted in their own small office he was impressed with Virgin's open-plan informality.

On the face of it, the deal they got with Virgin was not as good as some of the others they had been offered but it guaranteed the group what it needed most – freedom to develop at their own speed and in their own way.

Jon and Tony both had enough experience of the industry to realise that it was worth giving away a few points to ensure artistic independence. So, although they settled for a smaller advance and a smaller percentage of the profits than they could have creamed off some of the other companies, they gained the vital bonus of having total control over their songs.

Virgin arranged a photographic session for the band at which George – not for the first time in his life – kept being mistaken for a girl. In the past, it had not mattered too much but now he was about to launch himself on an uninitiated public he felt he should at least make it plain what he was – in name, at any rate. Practical as ever he added 'Boy' to his name. Boy George. It had the right ring to it.

George O'Dowd, the boy who would have died to be successful, had a band, an organisation, a recording contract and a new name. All he needed now was the success.

12 It's a Miracle

Culture Club's first record *White Boy* was released in May 1982, followed in June by *I'm Afraid of Me*. Both barely skimmed the surface of commercial recognition before sinking without trace. George and Jon felt that they had to keep churning out singles to grab the public's attention rather than space them out in the normal way. In September *Do You Really Want To Hurt Me?* dropped on the reviewers' turntables.

Their comments were scarcely encouraging. They ranged from "weak, watered-down, fourth division reggae" to "woefully ordinary . . . an unremarkable whinge with a soft underbelly". One of the music press writers described it as "lily-livered . . . overblown Motown" and added "it's plain that the group's only asset is the ludicrously unphotogenic Boy George. God help 'em!"

Do You Really Want To Hurt Me? had been a joint effort. It had been George's idea but it was Jon who suggested they played it as a lover's reggae song. Steve Levine polished up the sound, Roy wrote the keyboards and Mikey did the bass. The recording was done in one take with Jon and Steve doing the mixing together later. Said George at the time: "It's a song, written as a song, probably the only proper song we've got with proper chord sequences and keyboard changes in it. It's just very musical. I think it's a very well constructed song."

The public appeared to agree with him. By November *Do You Really Want To Hurt Me?* had arrived at the top of the British charts, going on to sell more than seven million copies worldwide. Suddenly, Culture Club existed as the musical force that George had envisaged.

The band was invited to go on television's *Top of the Pops*; after all those months of being just another face in the swirling crowd of professional fans, George was the star of the show.

In a modern semi-detached in suburban Kent, his old friend Jane, eight and a half months pregnant, sat watching the programme. "And all of a sudden, there was George. I was just so amazed I couldn't believe it," she says. "I just could not believe it. There was I sitting there, all married, pregnant and homely and there was he – being famous and earning lots of money.

"I knew him instantly although he looked more outrageous than when I'd last seen him and the style was different. But I knew the face straight away, and the voice, really."

She bought the record to commemorate the birth of her son, Alex, who now calls his mother's former playmate, Uncle George. At about the same time, George was telling interviewers: "It's like childbirth when you get to Number One, the relief and the ecstasy."

Now the initial labour pains were over George was determined that Culture Club should lose none of its momentum. "It never stops," said George after that first hit. "The band has to go on for ever until we get there. When do you ever get there?"

Certainly not after one hit record. George was delighted that *Do You Really Want To Hurt Me?* was judged on its musical merits rather than his sartorial eccentricities but, even so, it was now up to Culture Club to prove that they were more than one-hit wonders.

Their next two singles, *Time (Clock of the Heart)*, released in November 1982, and *Church of the Poison Mind*, released five months later, reached numbers three and two respectively in the British charts, but it was *Karma Chameleon* that installed the

band in the superstar bracket. Released exactly one year after *Do You Really Want To Hurt Me?* it went straight into the number two slot in the charts before moving up to number one where it stayed for six weeks. The song, according to George, is about "this terrible fear of alienation that people have, the fear of standing up for one thing. It's about trying to suck up to everybody – 'oh yes, I agree with you'. What we're saying in the song is, if you aren't true, if you don't act like you feel, then you get karma – justice. That's nature's way of paying you back."

Ironically, it could be said that Culture Club was trying to "suck up to everybody" with their melting-pot style of music. It defied all generalizations, crossed every acceptable pop boundary and challenged comparison with almost every known singer from Smokey Robinson to Gilbert O'Sullivan. "The aim is to be creatively fluid," says George, "to make everything we do a little different. We want to be a bridge between white rock and black soul."

He openly admits to plagiarism: "It's one of my favourite words. Culture Club is the most sincere form of plagiarism in modern music – we just do it better than most"; however, Jon insists that it is a case of "extension" rather than "imitation". "If everything's an imitation you never get anything new," he argues. "you can have music with its roots in soul but it's an extension of it. In Culture Club we play our own brand of soul, just as we play our own brand of reggae."

Certainly, the band geared itself to be unashamedly commercial. "That's the first thing George and I agreed on when we formed the group," says Jon. "We decided we were going to be a pop group which meant appealing to anyone who wants to listen and enjoy the music. We're entertainers, not politicians. We know what we want to do with the band and we'll do whatever is necessary to promote it. What's wrong with *Top of the Pops*?"

Making and breaking records

What indeed? Having been part of the Blitz elitist minority, George was well aware that he had to appeal to a far wider audience if he was going to produce hits.

"A lot of people think London's the only place in the world and that's the problem with a lot of these people who are extremely trendy," says George speaking from personal experience. "I've lost my trendy audience now. It's all gone to Marilyn which is all well and good. I don't need that audience. But, then, they were never really with me in the first place. I wanted to be commercial and the music I had was totally commercial. A lot of people think it's very easy to make a pop record. What they don't realise is that it's far easier to make a record for ten people than for ten million. That's a very hard thing to do. And you can never ever cultivate the perfect pop record – it's just pure luck."

Luck or not, their first album, *Kissing to be Clever*, released in October 1982, sold nearly five million copies in the first two years. Three of its tracks – *Time (Clock of the Heart)*, *Church of the Poison Mind* and *I'll Tumble 4 Ya* – reached the American Top Ten, something no other artist had managed since The Beatles. Their second album, *Colour By Numbers*, released one year later, went straight to the top of the charts and sold eight million copies in nine months. The *Times* reviewer described it as a "vivid collection of danceable, eminently memorable tunes, containing songs that concentrate on emotional quality rather than complex political issues" and compared the group "occasionally" to Motown greats like Stevie Wonder and Marvin Gaye. Culture Club's next two singles, *Victims* and *It's a Miracle*, got to numbers three and four in the charts respectively.

But it was the extraordinary success of *Karma Chameleon*, that took even Culture Club by surprise. They had written the song a year earlier and argued over whether it should actually be released as a single or not. Indeed, the first time Roy heard the number he thought it was dreadful. Luckily, George refused to take any notice of his opinion.

Theoretically always the egalitarian, in practice George's Irish temper was now coming frequently to the fore especially when it involved the band's creativity. It was regarded as a family matter, a volatile relationship that sparked off the inevitable bursts of acrimony. It flared up most noticeably between George and Jon – "both of us are very strong personalities with big egos" admits Jon. "We have terrible rows over practical matters when I think George's wild imagination is running away with him. He's a very emotional person who can be neurotic and bitchy although basically he's really kind and good-hearted."

Says George: "The good thing about this band is that we have four weeks writing together in a dingy little rehearsal room and then we argue, throw coffee over each other, smash guitars, swear and call each other obscenities. Then, when we get to the studio, we all work. We all do our arguing beforehand."

Their third album, *Waking Up With The House on Fire*, which they completed in August 1984 after their tour of Japan and Australia, was prepared with all the familiar signs of dissension.

"We booked two or three weeks to do the songwriting and didn't use one day of it," Jon recalls. "We had an argument and we left. We tried again three days later and had another argument. We rowed and rowed and George smashed his tape-recorder and I threw a chair at him. Then we wrote the album in four days."

On tour, stuck in each other's company for days – even weeks – on end, the four frequently let off steam by squabbling. Of them, George and Mikey are probably the least compatible although George has said in the past that he has little in common with any of the band. And he admits there was a time when his personal success brought the situation to crisis point. "The rest of the group had to stand behind me and had to put up with the heads of record companies coming up and shaking my hand and ignoring them." The internal pressures in the band nearly caused them to break up during the 1983 tour of Japan. Yet, ironically it is because they all have an equal say in the final result that the disagreements occur. And, having always had his own way and the last word in most arguments, it is hard for George

"A family situation"

to share the decisions – particularly when he believes he is right. For, despite his having always insisted that he wants a democratic band who are not simply "musos" but contributing members with minds of their own, both he and the band appreciate only too well that it is George who is the focal point of their success.

They all admit it has caused problems. At one stage, in the autumn of 1983, George even went so far as to announce that in future he would be leaving all the interviews to the band. "They're beginning to project themselves," he declared. "They're really coming out of themselves and becoming established stars." It never really happened because it was George in whom the media was interested and George, erudite and articulate, who could produce a dozen answers to any one question.

It was also George who won the personal acclaim. It might have been Culture Club who captured the awards for the Best Single of 1983 with *Karma Chameleon* but it was George who became the first person ever to be voted the *Daily Mirror's* Personality of the Year two years running, and George who has featured in the world's music press listings as both Best Male Singer and Best Female Singer.

And, although George naturally enjoys the personal recognition, he gets incensed if he feels that the band are denied their share of the credit. When the American organizers of the 1984 Grammy Awards expected George alone to collect Culture Club's award he was furious at what he considered a slight to the rest of the band. In retaliation he came out with his classic line: "Thank you America – you've got taste, style and you know a good drag queen when you see one." He later explained that he said it to get back at the organizers by being bitchy rather than bitter. Unfortunately, the Americans took the flip remark seriously and, while the university students spent hours analysing his motivation, their media have referred to him

as a self-acclaimed drag queen ever since.

The band say they have come to terms with the fact that George is the star. "We realise that it is very embarrassing for him that people tend to ignore the rest of the band," says Jon. "He thinks it isn't fair and so do we. But obviously he's going to get the attention because of the way he looks and the fact that he's a terrific character. The rest of us are trying to be sensible about it. Each one of us accepts our roles in Culture Club. We know that the band is a magical mixture and that if any one member decided to leave it would collapse. But George is the eye of the band, the media king and I'm the mechanics behind the music."

When *Karma Chameleon* became a world-wide best-seller it inevitably changed all their lives but George's life in particular. It was the point at which he moved from being a pop singer to a superstar. Suddenly, everything he did was front page news and the inevitable pressures forced him to become almost a recluse. It also made the whole band individual millionaires, creating pop history by achieving that stepping stone in the shortest time ever. Tony Gordon hired a team of financial experts to invest the profits, divided equally four ways, with each member of the group paying himself a weekly salary of £180.

It is difficult for all of them – and their families – to come to terms with the fact that they are now extremely wealthy young men. Roy likes to recount the story about the time when his father announced that the price of petrol was going up. "Who cares?" said Roy, to which his father, rocking with pleasure, responded: "It's good to hear a son of mine say that!"

It matters enormously to all four of them that their success – both the fame and their steadily growing fortunes – is due to their music and not just the gimmickry of Boy George. "You can't base a career on a gimmick," says George, before adding: "I honestly believe my personality is the most

Robert Mitchum decides to adopt George

**A sea breeze in Poole, Dorset,
nearly parts George from his lucky hat**

important thing about what I'm doing. It's more important than rock and roll, than anything." And he is the first to recognise the advantages of the package he has created. "It pleases me that my image doesn't quite fit with the music," he says. "I like the audience to have the impression that things aren't quite what they seem. I want to keep shuffling my cards.

"When I started I wanted people to look at me and say 'that guy's got no future' and then I wanted to go out and play for them just to prove that we *could* play. I wanted people to think that we were stupid so I could prove them wrong. And it worked perfectly."

But it worked perfectly only because George's instinctive feel for what the public wants both musically and visually is as unerring as was his ability to make himself into a celebrity without portfolio back in the days of Blitz; just as his decision to use Helen Terry as his co-vocalist brought new strength and depth to the Culture Club sound while taking away none of the spotlight from himself. Indeed, Helen, who had done session work and taught singing, contributed considerably to the band's initial musical success. George first met her when she was singing – fully clad – with the eccentric Neo-

naturists. He asked her to help record *Do You Really Want to Hurt Me?* and then invited her to become a full-time member of Culture Club. She eventually left to pursue a solo singing career.

Live, the combination of George's personality and obvious sense of fun, the band's professionalism and their easy-listening music, appeals both to the kids and their parents, causing one *Daily Telegraph* critic to enthuse gratefully that "almost alone among teenybop idols since The Beatles, Culture Club give a performance which can be enjoyed heartily by anyone". Certainly, a Culture Club concert assails all the senses, a spectacle of colour, movement and music. It is a complete entertainment, a *son et lumière*. And, the fact that about one-fifth of British audiences consists of over-forty-year-olds, emphasizes George's across-the-board appeal, an appeal which tends to endure. Another critic compared George to a "demented rabbi going hoppity skip to Grandmama's cottage" adding "strangely enough I thought Boy George was rather good".

And George *is* good. "He has a superb voice in the old-fashioned sense of having a good voice," says Britain's top disc jockey Mike Read. "He has a lasting quality in his voice and the other lasting quality is that he is interesting, witty and makes sense." And George Martin, The Beatles' record producer, agrees. "Boy George is one of the more memorable people of the new breed of talent. He has a much better voice than half the other singers around."

George, himself, believes that the "good, structured songs" have a lot to do with the band's success; also the fact that their live show is straightforward. "People anticipate. 'What's he going to come out wearing? A tutu with light bulbs all over it?'" But he adds: "I don't go in for any of that rubbish – Woolworth painting and glitter. I think you've got to rely on your own talent or fall flat on your arse. Singing is my main talent

but the dress is entertainment and the band looks colourful together."

It may sound simple and, on stage, George makes it look simple, but the slickness is applied as meticulously as George's make-up. "I believe a band is twenty-five percent talent and the rest is hard work," says George. "If you want to be a world artist you must really work hard for that and you must cultivate it all you can to make that work for you. I think the best businessman in the world is one who works twenty-four hours a day, not someone who stops at five o'clock and gets drunk. A lot of people look at me and say 'oh, he's just a dummy dressed up' and they forget what goes into it to make it tick. You do *have* to have talent but you also have to work hard with it. I think it did us a hell of a lot of good having those two flop singles initially. I think if we'd had a hit with *White Boy* we'd have gone a bit over the top."

As always seems to happen, Culture Club's phenomenal success has resulted in other record companies trying to get themselves a Boy George band to make their fortune, too. George does not regard such imitation as flattery. "It makes me sick," he says angrily, "because when I started in this business everyone looked at me and said 'give up, George, you're a joke.'"

13 Love Games

"**B**oy George – the lead singer for Culture Club and a man who describes himself as 'a good drag queen' – has found love with a gorgeous Japanese model named Mitsuke." So began an article in one of the more sensational weekly publications in the United States which went on to quote an anonymous source as saying: "Happiness has blossomed in his bizarre life. You might say Miko is instructing Boy George in the delicate art of oriental courtship. Miko has already moved into Boy George's London home." Another anonymous "insider" confirmed that the two "are inseparable. George has gone completely overboard for the Japanese way of life."

Confronted with a superstar of uncertain sexuality and with no obvious contender with whom to link his name, the American press had been driven to do a little match-making of their own on George's behalf. When George and Miko flew out of Heathrow Airport together, holding hands and both clad in ankle-length kimonos, it seemed a perfect opportunity to bring a little romance into their lives.

The reality was a little less newsworthy. "Miko is a dancer friend of mine," George had explained to reporters before he and Miko left for the music festival in San Remo. "I met her in Japan when she was working for a rock magazine. Now she's coming with me to liven up our stage show. We should turn a few heads."

They certainly did, the following day, when George prolonged the charade by giving Miko a long, lingering and very public

George and Miko – "I love her very much"

farewell kiss, in front of the incredulous Italian press. "I'll really miss her," announced George. "I love her very much. Miko has been very special to me since we met two years ago in Tokyo." For the record, he added: "We are not having an affair. There is nothing physical in it. But she is an intelligent person and my relationship with women requires that they have to be very intelligent and bright."

Earlier, at a press conference, an Italian reporter demanded to know whether George was homosexual. "That is not the point," said George looking fixedly at the questioner, a young man wearing heavy ear-studs and hip-hugging jeans. "That is a rude question. Because I dress exotically it does not imply that I'm a deviate. I am different. I am me."

Asked what exactly was her relationship with Boy George, Miko laughed and said: "We are just good friends – I think that is what you say".

It was certainly not what the American newspapers intended to say but, then, they were desperate. What was the point of having an exotic new pop phenomenon who appeared not to have a love life? What on earth were they to write about?

Later George went to the trouble to explain that his appearance at the airport with Miko had been carefully planned as a cultural statement rather than a sexual camouflage. "Miko's a friend. I'd have more chance of going out with a door!" he told one music magazine. But it was typical of George to use the Miko episode to cloud with ambiguity the whole issue of his sexuality. And he has created a similar veil of mystery around his relationship with two other close friends.

Before Miko, the media's money had been on Marilyn as the most likely object of George's affection. When the two arrived back from a holiday in Egypt together, the tabloids had a field day, inspiring the inevitable gags as to which one was Queen of the Nile. On the strength of that publicity Marilyn, at the time an aspiring singer himself, sold his exclusive story to *The Sun* under the headline "BOY GEORGE AND ME – BY MATE MARILYN. People think we're in love". Marilyn's revelations included the fact that "actually, I don't think George likes boys at all. What he really likes is being outrageous." And added: "Where I come from it's quite normal for mates to go on holiday together, especially when you haven't got a girlfriend."

Marilyn's "exclusive" infuriated George who refused to have anything more to do with him. "When I came back from Egypt with him I knew there'd be press but what was I to do – hide myself in a box?" demanded George. "I did it as a favour to him. I gave him the publicity because he needed it. But it wasn't enough for him to have that, he went on to do interviews about me. When I picked up *The Sun* and saw what he'd done it stopped our friendship. We were both very thirsty – I took him to the

George and Marilyn – "People think we're in love"

oasis and he drank the whole lot."

Marilyn, by now sitting on a recording contract of his own, sniped back in print. "George doesn't answer my phone calls any more. I reckon people surrounding him see my success as a threat and are turning him against me. I've known him for eight years as George O'Dowd who is witty, loving and talented. But now he's created this alien character called Boy George who's completely different to the guy I used to get on with. When George is nice he's wonderful – but when he's not it's the end of the world because he can be so harsh. I'm not going to

"A six-foot bloke with a body like Tarzan"

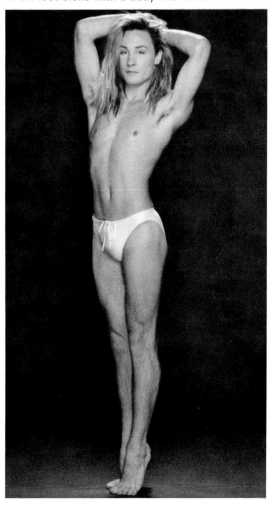

give up on finding the old George again, though." And, to settle the matter once and for all, he added: "George is not my type at all. He's sweet and a bit tubby but he doesn't turn me on. It's always been the furthest thing from my mind with him."

The rift between George and Marilyn continued for several months with the pair of them bitching at each other through mutual friends and the media. Marilyn was determined to renew their friendship and on one occasion went round to see George at his flat to attempt a reconciliation. "When George saw who it was at his front door he rowed with Marilyn for two hours and then decided not to let him in," revealed one newspaper. It all made good copy and doubtlessly helped to take Marilyn's first record, *Calling Your Name*, to number four in the charts.

By now, the blonde male siren was commanding almost as many column inches as his former friend. "I didn't really want to be photographed with Boy George, but what

Marilyn with photograph of "this alien character"

do you do?" complained Marilyn. "I certainly didn't need the publicity. A boy dressing up as Marilyn Monroe is quite a news item in itself so I really don't need anyone else's help. And negotiations for the record deal were already under way before we went away together." Ironically, it was Ashley Goodall, now A & R man with Phonogram, who signed the record deal after seeing him posing at Camden Place "looking like a star". George was not impressed with Marilyn's new image. "He's spent the whole of his life being Marilyn Monroe and now he's being Boy George and it's not true enough in a way. It stinks of being a record company product." And, privately, he refers sarcastically to Marilyn's "monster hit" as "Do You Really Want To Time Church".

The tiff gave both George and Marilyn an opportunity to sharpen their tongues on the other's reputation. "The trouble with both of them is that they are jealous of each other," confides someone who knows them well. "George is jealous because Marilyn is so beautiful – a lot of people think he's better looking than George. And Marilyn is jealous of George's popularity." Even when they *are* on speaking terms their pet names for one another are scarcely flattering. Marilyn calls George "Mr Doughnut" or "Fat Pig", and George calls Marilyn "Pigface" or "Failure". One of George's favourite lines is: "Shut up, Failure, go and have another flop!"

It was Philip Sallon who finally reunited the squabbling friends after a series of telephone calls one evening which he later recounted to another friend. It began when Philip rang George at his flat to tell him "Marilyn and Robert (*a friend of Marilyn's*) are here. Why don't you come on over."

"No," said George, slamming down the receiver. Five minutes later he rang back. "Who else is there?"

"Just Marilyn, Robert and me," said Philip.

"Oh, no. I'm not coming," said George, hanging up.

Five minutes later he rang Philip again.

"I'm coming over. Send Robert to pick me up."

The bitchy rivalry between George and Marilyn extends even into the hallowed realms of their alter egos. "Marilyn's really pretty but his projection is disgusting," ranted George to No. 1 magazine. "I think the sight of a six-foot bloke with a body like Tarzan who's built like the side of a house trying to be Marilyn Monroe is quite offensive."

George's own appearance was, of course, by now a matter for universal debate. He was justifiably annoyed when the public, comparing him to his childhood idol David Bowie, suggested that his clothes and make-up were part of his act. "The difference between me and Bowie is that he met people who made him weird whereas I've been weird from the beginning," he declared. Nor was he impressed by the fact that stardom had made him acceptable. "I'm discovering how hypocritical people are. When I wasn't famous and dressed like this, people were rude to me. Now that I'm successful they're fantastic. But I don't forget what happened in the past. It is acceptable to be an eccentric pop star and I hate that kind of approval. I think it's sick when people want to give you love just because you're a pop star."

And love, of one kind or another, was exactly what everyone wanted to give Boy George. His androgynous style meant that he could be all things to all people. Whatever their fantasy – Boy George fitted the bill. In the meantime, they wanted to know everything about him – from whom he slept with to where he bought his make-up. And while neatly side-stepping the former question, George was only too delighted to share his beauty secrets with anyone who was interested. "I've just shaved my eyebrows off again. I'm getting more like I was when you used to know me," he confided to one glossy magazine writer. "I'm really into smoky grey eyeshadow at the moment I use Clinique, Cosmetics à la Carte and an American brand called Make-up Studio. I don't pretend that I don't need make-up. I'm like Sheena Easton – she's like a plain egg without make-up on but when she's made-up she's so beautiful. I think make-up makes me sexy. Now that my hair's more natural I use heated curlers in it. I've also got some good French rollers, they're really big and make great quiffs. You can only get them in Paris though."

Such personal titbits, however, only served to whet the public's appetite for more intimate revelations. Indeed, the public is almost led to believe there are more intimate revelations to be made. Now we know what you wear on your face, tell us about your private life, George. But, of course, George has no intention of discarding the ambiguity he has created, not even when it comes to talking about his friendship with Jon Moss whom several of his friends believe is the closest person to him now.

And those who know George best believe that merely the way he glances at his good-looking drummer, even in public, tells all. As long ago as November 1982, one of the girls

from the Carburton Street squat asked him: "Are you still going out with Jon Moss?"

"I've never gone out with him," George snapped back.

"That's not what you told me two weeks ago," retorted the girl.

"I might have said that I love Jon but I didn't say I was going out with him," argued George. "But, then, I love all the band."

A year later it was Jon's turn to deny any romantic involvement with George. "The first time I met George I really fancied him," he told reporter Sharon Feinstein. "He was wearing make-up and outrageous clothes and I was struck by how attractive and sensual he was. He is also very charming and warm-hearted and that had an affect over me. I was amazed at myself for having those feelings for a guy. But George and I have never had a sexual relationship. And now we know each other so well that I don't think it could ever happen. I've never been to bed with a bloke but I certainly wouldn't discount it. I must be pretty broad-minded to be part of a band like Culture Club."

Certainly, Jon possesses the characteristics that George has fallen for in men in the

George and Jon – "best friends"

past. Jon is older by almost four years, attractive, manly and someone George can respect mentally. And although Jon is about six inches shorter than George, they "go well together", according to friends. George himself says: "Jon's far more sexy than I'll ever be. He's a beautiful guy and I think he should show the world that. I've always told Jon – 'you're too nice'. He's the good version of what I should be." And he once told a friend: "I think Jon's a much sexier person than Marilyn. He's got hairier legs and he's much more erotic."

It was Jon who expanded George's interest in the Jewish faith, which had already been kindled by Philip Sallon. Jon also gave him the Hasidic hat which George wore solidly for the first year or so of Culture Club's existence. George regards the hat as a lucky mascot and once, in Los Angeles, when it vanished in a surge of hysterical fans, it was Jon who retrieved it for him.

George has never tried to hide the fact that he and Jon are more than just members of the same band. "I'm very close to Jon," he has said. "I trust him more than anybody and he's probably my best friend, but by the same token I've got nothing in common with some of the things Jon does." In a separate interview he admitted: "Obviously, Jon's very special to me. We've always been really close."

During their autumn tour of Europe in 1983, George and Jon introduced their parents to one another in Nice. Jon's parents drove over from their home in Monte Carlo while George flew his mum and dad out for the weekend. They got on well despite their totally different backgrounds and lifestyles.

On tour, George and Jon frequently share a suite but they no longer travel regularly in the same car. In the past they would share one Mercedes while Roy and Mikey travelled in the other. These days, George is more likely to go in his own limousine while the three musicians ride together. And the increasing pressures on both their lives –

particular George's – have made it that much harder for Jon and George to go back to one another's homes for a late-night chat and a nightcap as they often did in the past.

Jon's reaction to George's personal success is typical of his caring attitude towards the younger man. "There was a time, I think, when he got – well, not carried away, but let's just say he might not have been in control of the situation. He was really being harassed from all corners. And it was hard on him. Now I find he's a better person because he's more secure in his success. He's confident now. He knows what he's good at. He has gone through a lot and he knows he can handle it."

Certainly, were it not for the fact that George is entirely secure about his own sexuality, he would have suffered something of an identity crisis during the early part of 1984 when he was voted top of both the Male and Female Sex Object categories by readers of a British music paper. He was also selected as one of the World's Ten Most Desirable Bachelors by the American-based International Bachelor Women's Society, along with Dudley Moore, Pierre Trudeau and Johnny Carson. Then, Richard Baker, the BBC presenter, accused him of "transvestite extravagances" on his live early-morning radio show, which caused George to collapse with a fit of the giggles while fellow guest, writer Tony Taylor, did his best to defend him. A few months earlier George had been attacked orally at a gay discotheque in Islington by a customer who thought he should be defending gays and objected to him using the expression "poof" in interviews. "I've been beaten up for wearing a Gay Pride badge," complained the man.

"I've been in trouble for wearing a Mother's Pride badge," quipped George.

He even fell out with his old friend Jeremy of Haysi Fantayzee over which of them had first worn dreadlocks. "I used to know Jeremy when he was a normal boy," jibed George. "He used to look like an accountant

but now he doesn't talk to me because he thinks I copied his hairstyle. I looked like this well before he did. It's pathetic, really." Jeremy refused to comment but his manager revealed that "Jeremy is very hurt. He finds it difficult to talk to George now."

With all the petty squabbling and in-fighting it is hardly surprising that George relies more and more on Jon's clear judgement and good common sense.

"As soon as I met George I realised he needed me," Jon has admitted. "Something clicked between us and I knew we could make it together. The thing I like about George is that he's very human. He's a bit podgy beneath all those clothes and he's got other little imperfections. George is sex with emotion and that's really what people want."

Even so, it is typical of George to try deliberately to tease the public with his extravagant gestures of affection for Jon. They frequently fool around in front of the cameras – yet their true relationship remains an enigma.

Perhaps George sums it up best when he says: "I'd never talk about anyone I love because I believe that people should be very loyal to each other and not talk about the other person.

"I don't believe in betrayal."

Fooling around in front of the cameras

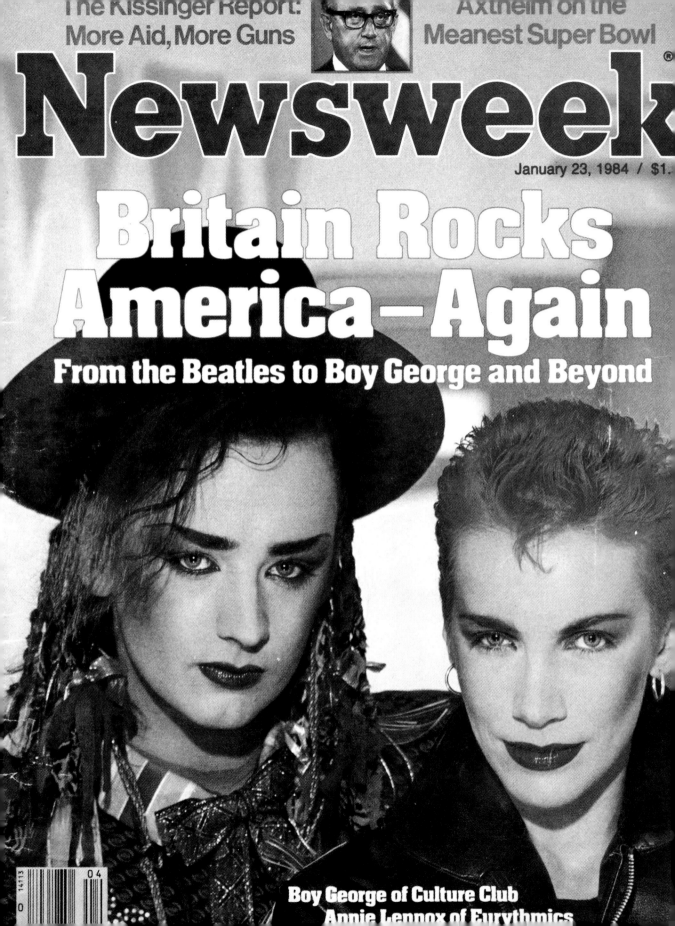

The Kissinger Report:
More Aid, More Guns

Axthelm on the
Meanest Super Bowl

Newsweek®

January 23, 1984 / $1.

Britain Rocks
America – Again

From the Beatles to Boy George and Beyond

Boy George of Culture Club
Annie Lennox of Eurythmics

14 *Culture to the Colonies*

*G*eorge's jet-setting life-style began when *Do You Really Want To Hurt Me* reached the top of the Belgian charts. Until then he had never left England – and had no desire to do so. Now, however, Virgin wanted Culture Club to fly out to Belgium to promote their first hit.

Still unsure as to the staying power of their latest chart-toppers, the record company flew them out on a "really cheap old plane." George hated it and would happily have never flown again. Today, several hundred flying hours later, he still hates it, finding it dull, uncomfortable and frightening.

Nor was he greatly impressed with Europe – either then or on subsequent visits. Parisians laughed at him because he ordered coffee with his meals instead of wine. The Dutch television station made fun of *Do You Really Want To Hurt Me?* by preparing the studio as if for heart surgery. And, in Germany, George was shocked by the open sexuality that confronted him, especially when he got trapped by a horde of women who kept "sticking their tits in my face and telling me to sign them." He also disapproved of the heavy drug culture in both Germany and Holland. Remembering two of the girls from his squatting days who had got deeply involved in drugs and moved to Amsterdam, he was upset by the laid-back hippies he found there. His appearance

automatically attracted the dopers who would stop him in the street demanding "Hey, man, got any skins?" And, when a girl in a German restaurant greeted him with an off-hand "hi" and thrust a huge plate of white powder in front of him, George was appalled. "The first thing you should do," he reproached her, nearly blowing the powder off the plate, "is say 'hello' properly." It was only when his highly amused band told him that the contents of the plate had been worth about £2000 that George realised that it was cocaine.

Even performing in Europe presented difficulties because, without the audience participation to which he was accustomed, George found it hard to relate instinctively to the kids. In France, where over a million copies of both *Do You Really Want To Hurt Me?* and *Karma Chameleon* were sold, hardly anyone bothered to turn up to the concerts. In Strasbourg only two hundred people came to see Culture Club perform. And, in Italy, the band played to an audience made up entirely of boys who sat down quietly and listened blandly to the music. When a few of Culture Club's British fans tried to liven things up by dancing in front of the stage, the Italians threw Coke cans and cigarette packets at them. "Not one person screamed at me," recalls George, "they just sat and

looked." The problem was that, in a strict Catholic country, the girls are not allowed out at night especially to pop concerts.

It is therefore scarcely surprising that George prefers performing in Japan and Hong Kong where Culture Club plays to ecstatic audiences of thousands. When he appeared on stage in Osaka wearing a white wedding dress complete with veil and bridal bouquet, the crowd went mad. Only the former clientele of Billy's remembered that Philip Sallon had done the same thing years before. And when George slowly and sensuously undressed Jon and Mikey on stage revealing their underwear plus skin-coloured cod pieces, the fans applauded hysterically.

Ironically, George's influence has made his Japanese fans revert to wearing traditional Geisha outfits to his concerts, along with Boy George look-alike costumes, rather than their conventional western-style clothes. For, in Japan, George – or Boyee Boyee, as they call him – is very big indeed. At the time of writing, Culture Club had had six smash hits in Japan and sold more than three million pounds worth of records. The fans adore George for a variety of reasons ranging from his catchy music to his "big face". They also appreciate his efforts to understand their culture. He has, however, a head start for in the traditional Kabouki theatre, the men wear make-up and dress as women. "It's funny," says George. "I'm taking their own ideas and giving them back."

In Hong Kong, George was struck by the "sweetness" of the people to whom he, of course, almost six-foot tall, looks larger than life. "It was weird," he said after his visit in 1983, "going 17,000 miles and still getting mobbed when I got off the plane. It was seven-thirty in the morning and I had no make-up on. I looked like a potato! And the papers still said I was 'heavily made-up'. I looked like a pig – in fact, I looked like two pigs!"

"No, you didn't," murmured Jon loyally.

But it is in the United States that Boy George has really made his mark. After a tentative start to his initial tour there at a small sophisticated New York club called The Ritz, George has been hailed as 'the biggest thing' to hit America since The Beatles. And he has the mass adulation of hysterical fans to prove it. Playing to packed auditoria, often holding as many as 17,000 people at a time, Culture Club roared into action and turned every concert into a fancy dress party night. The fans were rapturous. The east coast citadel fell. The west coast fell. All that remained was the bit in between, which included the bible-punching towns of the mid-west and the southern states.

George's chance to woo the straight-laced folks of Middle America came with an invitation to appear on that networked institution, *The Tonight Show*. One leading newspaper was so horrified at the prospect that it condemned George flatly as a "corrupter of Europe which is drowning in a tide of homosexuality – and George is now bringing it to the U.S". With that kind of promotional material, millions of viewers tuned in prepared to be disgusted. Instead, they saw George being his usual amusing, winsome, articulate self, sparring eloquently with the show's relief hostess, comedienne Joan Rivers, and altogether proving himself to be a regular kind of a guy, albeit one wrapped in a bedspread and plastered in make-up.

Even the staid *Los Angeles Times* compared his "daft androgynous aura" to that of a "1980s Tiny Tim . . . with a smile as disarming as a new-born pup". The conclusive accolade came when the prestigious weekly magazine *Newsweek* put George on its front cover under the headline "BRITAIN ROCKS AMERICA – AGAIN".

Encouraged by George's apparent success as a television personality in provincial America, Culture Club decided to do a tour of the heartlands. This time they included the less sophisticated cities like Buffalo,

Pittsburgh, Cleveland, St Louis and Nashville, Tennessee, the legendary home of country and western music. The reaction they received was nothing less than extraordinary. Even the blue-collar rednecks surrendered to this endearing fella dressed as a woman whom they accepted as the most recent in a long line of British eccentrics.

Boy George became a national hero and everyone wanted to get in on the act. Towns all over America and Canada ran Boy George look-alike contests, open, naturally, to all sexes. In Montreal, where Culture Club was welcomed by 3000 screaming fans after it became the first band ever to sell more than a million copies of an album in Canada, blackmarket concert tickets were selling for nearly £200. In Ottawa, where they played to audiences of more than 20,000, hairdressers were charging £25 for a special Boy George hair-do. In Detroit, disc-jockey Dick Purtan started his own Boy George Fan Club for people who enjoyed Culture Club's music but could not bear to look at its lead singer. The free fan club kit included a mask to cover your eyes while you listened to Culture Club, a blank white button (so that nobody knew you were a club member), a copy of lyrics to the club's theme song, *If This Is Culture, Give Me A Club*, and a photograph of macho-man Clint Eastwood. In Milwaukee, a local group made their own spoof recording of *Karma Chameleon* which went "I'm a I'm a I'm a Milwaukean. . ." and resulted in Virgin Records threatening to sue them unless they agreed to give all profits from the record to leukaemia research. In Brooklyn, a leading psychiatrist claimed that Boy George mania heralded a huge sexual revolution. "Women today don't want to feel dominated or overpowered," said Dr Pietro Pinto. "They may swoon and sway and idolise but they want men who are not threatening. Also, girls are tending to swap roles."

And through it all, George stayed a virtual prisoner in his hotel suite, surrounded by an army of security guards, too scared of the

hysterical fans and any potential nutters with firearms, to venture further afield, writing letters and postcards to his family, friends and fans, scribbling out lyrics on scraps of paper and ringing home for a chat with his mother.

And so the phenomenon roared its way across the North American continent, gathering hysteria and social significance as it went, escalating into something bigger and much more "meaningful" than the musical force that George had originally envisaged.

And thus it was with the rest of the world also. Whether they condoned or condemned him no country seemed able to ignore Britain's most outrageous export. In Kuala Lumpur, the Islamic national television service cut George out of its screening of the Grammy Awards because of his "feminine face and attire" while sixty million magazine readers in nine European countries voted Culture Club their top pop group. George even won the hearts of the Australian he-men by announcing firmly "I'm no poofter!" But when he asked the Russians for permission to do a concert tour of the Soviet Union he received a very swift refusal from the Kremlin who feared he would corrupt the country's youth.

There is no question that George does present a dilemma overseas where many people are still not sure whether to laugh or cry at the image he presents. Certainly, he ran into trouble when he arrived at Nice airport where the immigration officials took one look at his passport photograph and one look at George and decided there was no way the two were the same person. "Here," said the inspector, jabbing a finger at George's passport, "you are pictured as a man. But here," and he indicated George with his heavy make-up, flowing hair and fetching pale blue kimono, "I see you as a woman." Whereupon he refused George permission to enter France.

It took three hours of unfriendly persuasion by George, his entourage and the

British press, before French officialdom caved in. The harrassed official explained: "You must understand I am only carrying out orders. In France, immigration officials do not allow in transvestites. I have to follow rules."

Even so, despite the hold-ups, hassles and aggravation of travelling as a way of life, George still gets a kick out of actually performing overseas. After his 1984 American tour he told his father: "I really enjoyed it, dad. It was lovely." The disarming understatement was typical of George's matter-of-fact approach to his awesome success.

Osaka

George's bridal gown
which drove the
Japanese wild
Inset: Flashback to
Philip at Billy's
six years earlier

The A-Team. back row, L to R: Debbie, Jon, Andria, Carole, Margo, George, Irene, Laura and Ida. Front row,
L to R: Roy, Melanie, Josey, Mikey, Patsy and Fleur

15 The A-Team

At the Red Bus Studios, just off the Edgware Road in north-west London, a handful of girl fans is hanging around outside, waiting for a glimpse of whichever pop star is the object of their particular desires.

Melanie, Margo and Fleur are chatting together as some local girls walk past and start jeering at Melanie's scarlet hair. The second time it happens Melanie flares up and lets fly with some home-spun abuse of her own. One of the heftily-built girls spins round.

"Just you come here and say that again."

"If you want to hear it again you'll have to come here," retorts Melanie. After another exchange the local girls vanish to return, minutes later, brandishing enormous metal poles. Now they stand, waving them threateningly, at Melanie, Margo and Fleur who scream as they try to fend off their attackers with bare hands.

Suddenly, a tall man appears wearing lipstick and a shapeless jacket. He grasps one of the poles and tries to force it away from the girl. "You don't need that. Put it down."

"No!"

Frozen with terror, Melanie watches the girl try to raise the pole to strike the man's face.

"I said 'put it down!'" he shouts.

Slowly the girl lowers her weapon and then lets it drop. It hits the ground with a clang. Temporarily defeated, she leads her gang away. Without another word the man turns on his heels and stomps back inside the studio.

After the recording session is over he stops to speak to Melanie and her friends.

"Right," says George. "You three go straight home. I don't want you hanging around here because those girls are wicked bitches and they're going to get you back."

Then he slides into his waiting limousine and is gone.

Melanie, Margo and Fleur belong to the most exclusive group of pop fans in the world. Christened the A-Team by George himself, the group consists of about a dozen girls who have built up a remarkable relationship with Britain's leading band.

They are not traditional groupies, swapping sexual favours for a brief encounter of any kind and a signed photograph of their idols. Nor are they the conventional bunch of starstruck teenagers to be found the world over clamouring around stage-doors. The relationship that these ten girls have with Culture Club transcends the normal barriers of fan idolatory. It is, quite simply, a lively and loving two-way friendship which, in many ways, is as important to the band as it is to the girls.

It started with four of them – Andria, Laura, Patsy and Debbie. Andria spotted George in Manchester not long after the group was formed. "You're the first person who's ever recognised me in the street," George told her. "Come and meet my band." The other three started writing to him after going to some of the Culture Club gigs.

"To be honest, I thought they were really young kids of about twelve or thirteen," admits George. When he eventually met them after the release of his first single he was astonished to discover that Patsy and Laura were a couple of years older than him while Debbie was about the same age as himself.

In those days, he and the band were grateful to the girls for "really gunning for us". Always a keen letter writer, George replied to all of their missives with light-hearted notes decorated with squiggles and drawings, and he always sent them long letters after every tour thanking them for going along. When Culture Club went on its initial American tour at the end of 1982, the band arrived at their first venue to discover Patsy and Debbie waiting for them. "I do not believe this," said George. "I just do not believe this." On alien territory themselves, he and the boys were delighted to see a couple of familiar faces in the crowd, "a little bit of England", as Jon puts it. But that was just the beginning.

Over the months ahead Culture Club was to be continually astounded by the determination and dedication the girls displayed and the dangers and hardships they endured on its behalf. Nothing, it seemed, would stop them following the band. Individually, they have spent literally thousands of pounds of their earnings, savings, borrowings and dole money to go on tour with Culture Club. They sleep rough, hitch rides, freeze, starve and end up drenched, just to be near the group. For its part, the band frequently gives them food and money, the occasional lift and a rare hotel room. "I don't encourage it," says George. "I won't encourage it. There are certain things I won't do." When Patsy's suitcases were stolen in America he was adamant that the band should not pay her fare home. "Either you pay or I pay," he told Jon. "I've paid already," said Jon.

When Andria ran out of money in Europe, the band gave her £100 to "spend on food and nothing else". When Irene fell down some steps at the theatre in Brussels, ripping the curtains, George made up a song about it to help her feel better and sang it to her for the rest of the tour. In Hamburg, when Patsy lost her handbag with her passport in it, the band got in touch with the British consul and gave her money to get home. "She was crying her eyes out," says George, "and I said 'enough. I'm sending you home if I have to drag you to the airport'." One week later, Patsy reappeared in Paris for the final two

Andria – "if he swears at us we swear back"

Margo and Melanie – £100 on a birthday present

concerts of the tour.

But most of the time the girls are on their own, suffering discomforts that George admits he could not tolerate himself. In Derby, five of the girls slept huddled against a wall in more than four degrees of frost. In Cardiff, Patsy spent the night walking three times round the town while the others slept in the freezing railway station. In Nice, they got thrown out of the foyer of the band's hotel at three o'clock in the morning and spent the rest of the night sitting in the entrance to an apartment block in the pouring rain. Hitching through the night between Amsterdam and Hanover, Laura and Debbie had to fight off the advances of an amorous Dutchman and then – horror of horrors – arrived late for the concert. In Glasgow, Melanie and Andria spent the night in a public lavatory "so hungry and frightened we couldn't even cry".

"You're mad!" George tells them constantly. "You're crazy – the lot of you!"

"But we can tell he's pleased, really," say the girls.

They love him as a friend, fancy him as a lover, but most of all regard him as an "ordinary" human being who accepts their shortcomings and takes the time and trouble to be nice to them.

Just as at school it was George who chatted to the old ladies and took home the lame ducks, so now he has found another group of individuals in need of affection. And the main reason why they adore him is because George, having always had a complex about his own body, is not bothered by superficial beauty. "I know when I go out on stage I don't look fantastic like my pictures, and the kids know that," he says. "They understand that we're not dealing with perfection. They know that what we're dealing with is real. I'm fun. I walk out on stage and say 'when you put your fairy on the Christmas tree, think of me!' My attitude is that there are a lot of people who have a good giggle at my expense. Great. The kids understand that

Jon at Heathrow Airport with a posse of fans

Andria with Mikey – "it's like a family"

and they know that to me they're all gorgeous."

Certainly, the A-Team are the first to admit that none of them would win a beauty contest. Yet they are all attractive in their own way. Especially to George. "If I fancied a boy when I was at school it would be a miracle if he said 'hello' to me," says Laura, "but George pays me more attention than any other bloke has in my life. He's the only man I've ever been able to talk to and I can say what I like to him. I don't think of him as a pop star. In fact, I hate him being a pop star because I resent all the other fans. I just think of him as George and that's it."

George himself is aware of the responsibility he carries with their affection. "I realise that we are in a position where we inspire people to do things," he admits. "We cannot just go out and say 'I've got no responsibility'. Of course, we have. I appreciate that one hundred percent and I do whatever I can."

At the start of Culture Club, Jon was sceptical about the lengths to which George went to keep in touch with individual fans. "He used to tell me I was crazy," says George, "but now he understands why I do it. Because if you don't develop a relationship with them it's like having a marriage and never talking. And we have got a relationship whether we like it or not."

It is an attitude held by the whole band, all of whom have formed their own links with the girls in the A-Team. Jon, in particular, is very involved with them and writes to them regularly. He also gets concerned about them. "Of course, I worry about them, but what can you do?" he says. "You can maybe look after two or three but then it grows to ten and then twenty. You can't look out for all those people. All you can do is advise them. It worries me to hear they've slept out but we can't put some of them up in hotels and not the others. It isn't fair. But I always try to make sure they're eating properly and that they get into the concerts."

It is this genuinely caring attitude on the part of the band that endears them even more to the members of the A-Team. When Margo and Melanie went round to George's flat one day to tell him they were going on his British tour, he told them: "Make sure you've got warm clothes". On the motorway he spotted their car with the luggage on top of it outside a café and stopped to stick a note on the windscreen, saying: "WATCH YOUR LUGGAGE! WHAT IF IT RAINS? PUT IT IN THE CAR!"

"It is like a family," admits George. "The A-Team are special to me but I will not be seen to be treating them any differently in front of the other fans." He makes a point of never inviting any of them into his home, nor will he telephone them. He was furious with Jon for ringing one of the fans to wish her a happy birthday.

On tour, however, he always sends individual letters and postcards to the girls at home, full of private jokes and personal messages. ". . .someone threw a banana at me," he scribbled from America. "Oh – it was plastic – you can imagine what I did with it! I threw it back. . ." To another fan he wrote ". . .flabby bums and swimsuits are in, hair out of dreadlocks – frizz. Wot – hasn't Boy George got a wife? . . ." When Patsy went to the band's television show in Paris he wrote to her ". . .you're crazy to go to Paris for a television show but we all hope you got home safe. Thanks for your support on all the tours – you're some trooper . . . see you soon, baby mad girl. Love George. PS You're appreciated!" He sends all the girls Valentine's cards and, occasionally, even parcels of assorted nicknacks from abroad, frequently forgetting the customs duty. One parcel he sent from Japan cost the recipients £40 to retrieve it.

He is well aware how any sign of favouritism on his part can have dramatic results, with the girls quarrelling among themselves and with him. After he once suggested that Patsy was probably the band's

favourite fan she received threatening phone calls from other fans. And it took half an hour to set up the photograph of the girls with the band because of the delicate negotiations over who should stand next to George. The sight of George holding hands with Miko caused such furious jealousy among certain members of the A-Team that it almost set back Anglo-Japanese relations by several centuries.

George does his best to placate the girls while preserving his independence. "Right!" he swore, after one outburst of in-fighting. "I'm never going to talk to you lot again! I don't mind if you hate each other – I'll give you the knives and you can kill each other!" But, as with most family tiffs, they are swiftly forgotten. By George, at any rate. For the girls, a single word of rebuke from him can result in days of suffering and sleepless nights. And George, being sharp-tongued, impetuous, and mercurial, can and quite often does unwittingly inflict pain.

"Sometimes he can be pretty nasty to us," confides Melanie. "Sometimes he says wicked things and it hurts, but he doesn't mean it. He does it to make a point. I think some of us are a bit naive and can't accept that he wants to be on his own sometimes. Margo and I have started to realise that and we don't hang around any more."

The girls bake cakes for George and make him clothes. When Margo and Melanie sent him a jar of cookies he sent them back a photograph of it standing on his kitchen shelf. George writes to their mothers and always makes a point of wooing them, too, when they come to his concerts. "You have to give love to receive it," he says, and even after all these years it is clear he still craves it himself. When Margo 'n' Melanie, as he calls them, got in a huff because they thought, wrongly, he had forgotten to write to them from America, he sent an extra letter around to their flat by motorbike messenger. "We felt so guilty that we dashed out and bought him a basket of fruit," says Melanie.

She and Margo spend all their spare money on George. Melanie works as a telephone booking clerk for a holiday firm, Margo takes the room service orders for a big hotel. She took the badly-paid job because the short hours mean she can spend the afternoon outside the studio when George is recording. She and Melanie share a council flat in south-east London which they have transformed into a Boy George shrine. Every wall is papered with posters and photographs of George and every room is crammed with Culture Club memorabilia. Their prize possession is one of his dreadlocks which they found in an ashtray in the recording studio and which they display next to a drumstick which once belonged to Jon. And, as with all love affairs, their very happiness depends entirely on George's moods. A smile from him sets them up for weeks. A sharp word and they flounder in despair. "In the early days, we'd get very excited about seeing him and go mad if he didn't give us a kiss," says Melanie. "But now it's all on a much more friendly basis. He'll say 'hello' and chat to us and then say – 'give me a goodbye kiss'." It is reminiscent of the "lovely hugs and cuddles" that Jane remembers so well from Louise's and the Black Prince days.

For his twenty-third birthday, Margo and Melanie spent £100 on a present for George. They had his horoscope done and bought him a dressing-gown monogrammed in silk, a bottle of Champagne and a laundry basket full of little personal items to take with him on his tour of Japan. They checked George's current whims with his personal assistant, Bill Button, and got him some black cotton knickers, white cotton socks, minty gel toothpaste, baby oil and baby shampoo and cotton buds, and a couple of make-up brushes which they traced to a fancy dress hire shop near Trafalgar Square after sneaking a look one day in his cosmetic bag. A few weeks earlier they had spent another £60 buying him a cotton jacket and matching

Bill Button scolds the fans for spending so much money on his boss

sweat shirt which they wrapped up in a little cane briefcase which he carries everywhere. "It melts our hearts and brings tears to my eyes when I see him with it," says Melanie.

Bill came round to their flat to collect the birthday present. "You're mad spending all that money on George," he scolded them and Melanie explained: "We work for our money, we saved for it – so why not? We like spending it on George. We're doing it because *we* get pleasure out of it, too."

The following day Margo and Melanie went over to the studio to wish George 'happy birthday', the day before he left for Japan. He arrived in his brown Rover, took one look at them and exploded. "It's ridiculous! It's not on!"

"What's not on?" demanded Malenie, dazed.

"You lot. Here. What are you doing here, anyway?"

Close to tears, Melanie nearly blurted out: "What do you think we're doing here? You're going out of the country tomorrow, this is the last day we'll be able to see you for two months, what do you think we're here for?"

Instead, she said: "George, how can you say that to us because you know damn well we never hassle you."

"I suppose you'll be at the airport tomorrow," snapped George.

"Not if you don't want us to," retorted Melanie.

"It's all right," said George, calming down. He smiled. "You two – you've bought me a beautiful present. I can't believe it. You've been so sweet." He stood chatting, aware of how much he had hurt them, and they parted friends. At the airport, the following day, he shouted to them: "I've got your knickers on, you know!"

Melanie makes excuses for his sudden burst of temper. "He'd had four big injections for Japan and he's really frightened of injections and you could see he was really in pain. . ." but a week later she and Margo were still agonizing over it. "We can't puzzle it out," she said. "It still hurts because he's never ever spoken to us like that before. I know he was ill but there was still no need to say that. We've never ever hassled him or jumped on him and we couldn't. And if he says 'go' we go. We see him shouting at the fans a lot – he really does. He gets really angry with them. But he's never shouted at us before."

But, even though Margo and Melanie may find it hard to accept, this is just George being George. Success has not transformed him into a monster despite the enormous pressures he now has to bear and he is on no more of an ego trip than he has ever been. He is simply behaving as he always has – as in the days when he would flare up and scream at his parents, storm out of the house and be back five minutes later offering to make them a cup of tea. George has always taken it for granted that you have big rows with the people you love. "I'm one of those people who doesn't know how to stop," he admits. As his mother says "George's temper is like a puff of smoke and once it's gone up – that's it. He'll very seldom hurt anybody – he just

sort of shouts a lot. Then he'll see that you're hurt and calm down." The difference is that real families take tantrums in their stride while George's newly-acquired extended family take them to heart.

Arriving home at his St John's Wood flat one day with Jon he discovered Margo and Melanie on the doorstep covered with whitewash. "I screamed at them," recalls George, "and then they said sheepishly 'we've painted your wall' and I said 'Oh God – I feel such a pig, you know exactly how to hurt people don't you!' They understood." In fact, the two girls had carried out their ad hoc decorating to cover up graffiti left by a group of uninitiated fans. Even George's disapproving middle-aged neighbour was so impressed that she made them both toasted sandwiches. George wrote the girls a thank-you letter the following day.

This merging of his professional and personal life is something that George finds hard to accept. By nature rather a private person – he will not allow even Bill Button to see him half-dressed – he resents the intrusion into his privacy while recognising its inevitability. "What I say to the girls is 'when I'm working – come' because I know they're part of my career and my working life. And I try to explain to them that if a boy fancied them and sat outside their house, they'd be furious, and they giggle and they go 'we wouldn't mind' and I say 'well, I'm not accustomed to it'. They throw jokes in my face but basically they're very sweet and they understand."

It is at times like this that George's philosophy pays off. Because he has built up a one-to-one relationship with his fans he can present them with logic while others might resort to force or abuse.

One morning, coming out of his flat at about 7.30 to buy a newspaper, he found two girls sitting on the step. "No!" he shouted at them angrily. "No way! It's freezing – you're going to die of cold! Go home!" A couple of days later he got a letter from them saying:

Studio stake-out

"You're a real pig. . . you're horrible – we can't believe it. . . Jon's much nicer than you are. . ." Anyone else would probably have thrown the letter away but George wrote back immediately. "I will not have you sitting outside my house in below zero temperatures," he chided. "I will not be responsible for you freezing outside my home. If you want me to act like a fake and pretend to be something I'm not then I'd let you stay but if you want me to act like a human being I'm going to tell you to go home. It's not on." The girls wrote back saying "O.K. you're not just a piece of furniture. We understand how you feel."

It is, perhaps, ironic that George, the rebel who spent his own childhood resisting authority, should now be in the position of having to inflict a form of discipline on his fans. Characteristically, however, he bases his on logic. Even so, he admits that "it's very

difficult to tell people not to do something they want to do. If we tell them not to come to a gig they just think we're being horrible. It's not just difficult to discourage them, it's absolutely impossible." And, having always done what he wants to do himself, George appreciates that quality in others. "It's impossible to say to people – 'stop doing it'. You just break hearts – and I'm not in the business of breaking hearts."

And, although the whole band regards the indefatigable A-Team with a mixture of affection and amusement, it is George who gives the orders. It was George who instructed their tour manager, Gary Lee, not to allow the fans to be "roughed up"; it was George who kicked up a fuss in Japan because of the heavy security in the stadium – "Culture Club fans don't hit each other, they're not violent, they don't pull out each other's hair"; and it was George who sent out three of his assistants after one of their American concerts to scour all the city's bus stops for Patsy who "looked like she was going to die" but refused to go home.

"Yes, I do cause a lot of trouble for myself," agrees George. "Sometimes we'll come out of a hotel and Gary will say 'get in the car' and I'll insist on stopping to talk to the fans. O.K. – it makes us late but it's not in my nature to be obnoxious."

He is, however, not immune to capitalising on the influence he wields over his devoted followers. At the start of one overseas tour he told them he was going to wear pink to the airport and instructed them all to do the same "to give the press something to think about". Most of the fans turned up obediently dressed in pink while George arrived late and cross and wearing his blue and grey kilt. Even so, the fans insist, George just wants to be treated like a normal person. "If he swears at us we swear back at him," says Andria. "He doesn't want to be treated like a star."

They are fiercely protective of him, and are often reduced to tears if they feel he is being harrassed by either photographers or fans. They even enjoy his quirks, like his habit of forgetting to return their pens, and the way he always covers himself up "although he's got a really beautiful body". The world has yet to view Boy George's arms and legs. And when it comes to tracing the whereabouts of George and the band, the A-Team's ingenuity knows no bounds. They have found out his addresses through post marks, car number plates and even his local launderette. They once discovered where Jon lived from a bill sticking out from under his car radio. And, when they arrive in a strange town, it takes them approximately two phone calls to find out the secret hideout where Culture Club is staying. "They ought to put them in M15," says Jon.

George delights in their perseverence – even when it conflicts with his tour manager's carefully laid plans. Sneaking out of a hotel through the back door one morning the band was thwarted by the A-Team tearing round the corner to meet them. "I burst into hysterics," says George, "because it was like Gary's little master plan and they'd ruined the whole thing. I screamed with laughter and grabbed hold of the lot of them and said 'great!' and they are great."

Yet although the girls know everything about Culture Club, the band knows virtually nothing about them. For, despite Laura's admission that she can say what she likes to George, few of the A-Team ever unburden themselves to the band. "I think it's a form of respect," says Jon. "They don't want to tell us where they come from or how they get the money to tour. I don't think they want to talk about their problems. I think they come with us to get away from them and that's what they enjoy. When you're with people you love being with – and we love being with them – you don't think about your problems. You celebrate being with them."

And, as with all families, even George's personal friends get involved with the A-Team. Philip Sallon, much admired because he and George "could be each other they're so alike" once took three of the girls out to George's favourite Chinese restaurant in North London. And Marilyn, who is rather envious of the girls' devotion to George, invites them into his flat and proceeds to "slag George off". Once it go so bad that Melanie refused to talk to him all evening. As the girls were leaving, Marilyn apologized. "I'm sorry, Blanche (*George's pet name for her*), I love my sister, really." George, however, also takes any opportunity to make bitchy cracks at Marilyn's expense, even telling the girls filthy jokes about him.

It is scarcely surprising that the girls regard George not only as a friend and surrogate lover but as a social occasion and even a way of life. "It's become like a syndicate," says George, "because the girls meet each other through the band. They write and thank me for helping them to meet so-and-so. It's like the Culture Club mafia."

Certainly, their fanaticism attracts the girls to each other, often to the exclusion of the outside world. "Yes, I am jealous of the other girls," admits Laura, "but at least we have something in common. The women at work tell me 'you can't love a pop star. You're living in a dream world.' A dream world – at my age! I'm twenty-four, not fifteen. It makes me sick – they just don't understand."

And Andria says: "George gives people a lot of confidence. He tells you truthfully if he likes your hair or not. Even if I get married and have a family, George will always be there. You can't spend so much time – and so much money – on someone and then just forget all about them. I can't imagine life without George."

By now, too, it may well be hard for George to imagine life without the A-Team. They have become a part of the Culture Club package, a vital ingredient of the band's success. And, at every Culture Club concert, before he goes out in front of the screaming fans, George always asks Gary the same question.

"Are the girls all right?"

16 *Paper Boy*

Dina O'Dowd answered the telephone in the hallway of the family home in Shooters Hill. It was George, calling transatlantic from Washington DC.

"You've been a naughty boy," scolded his mother down the phone, "swearing at photographers like that. You should be ashamed of yourself."

"Look, mum, you don't understand," said George, reverting to the most familiar phrase of his childhood. "It was seven o'clock in the morning and I don't want to sit there putting make-up on my face at that time of day. I got to the airport and I said to the photographers 'do me a favour – no photographs'. And they went – 'Oh, go on, George.' And I said 'when I come back I'll ring you first and you can take all the photos you want but I'm tired.' And what they do, mum, is get right up close so no one else can hear and say 'you're getting a right flash bastard.'"

"And I know my Georgie," says Dina, recounting the conversation, "he'd fly off the handle and swear at that. And he must have been really tired because he was here sewing the sequins on his costumes until about three o'clock in the morning." Add to the fact that George usually arrives at airports tense and grumpy and you have the conditions for fiery confrontation. However, the photographers who were, after all, only doing their job, had the headline writers on their side. "NAUGHTY BOY GEORGE" remonstrated the *Daily Mirror*, unknowingly echoing his mother's words.

In Washington, for the start of the band's second American tour, George explained the reason for his outburst. "People think I just sit around on my backside all day eating grapes. But I've worked very hard for what I've got and I value my privacy . . . Being photographed all the time is boring, boring, boring. How many times can you be photographed in a paper just for catching a plane? It's ridiculous. . ."

Maybe. But George was underestimating both his own popularity and the British media's unquenchable appetite for anything new on Boy George – if only the fact that he is about to get on a plane. George has come a long way from the days when his ambition was to be in every single newspaper in the country. Now he wants publicity on his own terms rather than when it suits Fleet Street. "All you want is my face," he shouted at Heathrow Airport. "I rose to fame on my voice." Which begs the inevitable question: would Boy George be as popular as he is if he did not look as he does? For many, the simple answer would be 'no'. And, the fact that George belongs to a tiny group of international superstars who are neither media products nor publicity hypes, scarcely entitles him, now that he is famous, to utilize the media purely as a publicity outlet.

Besides, the press relies on the unplanned and there is always going to be that unofficial shot snatched when least expected. That is something with which celebrities must learn to live. Yet, when a cameraman from one of the tabloids caught George shopping without make-up during the January sales, the singer behaved like a petulant prima donna, hitting him over the head with his umbrella and screeching "don't you dare take a picture of me!" And when one of his former friends sent one of the newspapers an old early-morning photograph of George during his squatting days looking like a washerwoman, he was furious. Indeed, George has instilled a sense of nervous loyalty in many of his friends as far as talking about his past is concerned. One music press reporter, who spoke to George's old friends about his quick temper and bitchy tongue, recalls that everyone he interviewed was

"literally trembling – as if I was doing a story on a gangland leader rather than a pop singer". George later admitted that "most of the article was true. But everybody has that side to their character."

Right from the start of Culture Club, George has waged a personal crusade against the music press who have criticised the group. "When the band started it was so *obvious* to slag us off," he says, "but it's just pathetic. Who needs it?" Adding: "I think creative criticism is an art and destructive criticism is a waste of time" which may be true in a perfect world but is, sadly, unrealistic in this one. When a *Melody Maker* reporter told him "your music leaves me cold" George was livid. "I thought it was totally ridiculous," he says. "I don't see the point of interviewing somebody you don't like." Even so, everyone is entitled to his or her own opinion.

And the fact remains, whether he likes it or not, that George is the media personality of the moment and, as such, he must take the bad with the good – although the vast majority of the press he receives is favourable – if not adulatory.

Agony auntie Marje Proops with the "object of my adoration"

Even Marje Proops, the redoubtable doyenne of Fleet Street's agony aunties, fell in love with George when they met. "If anyone had said to me that the object of my adoration in 1984 would be a 22-year-old male called O'Dowd who wears heavy make-up, ribbons in his hair and nice dresses, I'd have advised them to get a head examination," she gushed. "But here I am, one of the adoring fans and feeling unbelievably special, would you believe it, because this George O'Dowd hugged me and told me he loved me."

And, whatever else he is or is not, George is good copy, if only because he has an answer to everything. So much so that one of the tabloids carried a page full of his perfectly commonplace opinions under the inflated headline "THE WISDOM OF BOY GEORGE". It was of interest only because the public and the press expect George's ideas to be as outrageous as his appearance. The fact that they are not makes news.

And, since he freely admits that he dresses as he does to attract attention, perhaps it is asking rather too much of the media to expect them to switch off the attention when it does not fit in with his own plans. Besides, George enjoys being controversial. When he compares himself to Princess Diana he knows very well it is going to make the headlines.

Certainly, the newspapers take advantage of every opportunity to use pictures of George in their columns. When *Karma Chameleon* was at number one in the charts and selling 95,000 copies a day, one Sunday paper ran a competition asking its readers to tell them what Boy George wore in bed. To avoid possible embarrassment it added the footnote "...don't take the question too seriously, please!"

It is unlikely that anyone would, simply because George's appearance does not inspire seriousness. And that is where the anomaly lies. George expects to be judged as the intelligent human being he undoubtedly is rather than the archetypal oddity he

The stars get in on the act: footballer George Best and comedians Ronnie Corbett and Kenny Everett get the Boy George treatment outwardly appears to be. Only his conversation stands between him and condemnation in the eyes of the middle-of-the-road public. And George himself is well aware of the fact, which is why he appreciates the potential power of television. "I can't wait to go on chat shows," he admits, scorning stars like Sting and Simon Le Bon who profess to dread them. "I love them. They are a chance to project your personality, to show people that there is a reason for liking you as well as your songs." Smart thinking – and, once again, it is George utilising the media to his own advantage.

But, however much he succeeds in controlling some of the publicity he receives, not even George can manage to manipulate it all. There is always going to be at least one journalist who will elect him "Wally of the Week" or "that girl with the great voice". When it actually happened, in the early months of Culture Club, George had the wit to recognise it as being "all good publicity". In those days, he needed it, and it was partly the result of that and the subsequent media coverage he received that he became the world-wide phenomenon he is today. It was the newspapers who dreamed up popular labels like "gender bender" and "unisex hero", tangible handles for an incredulous public to grasp.

Even the normally urbane *Times Educational Supplement* ran a lofty six-week exchange of correspondence debating the rights and wrongs of George's expulsion from school. George's old headmaster, Peter Dawson, joined in what he described as the "hilarious hullabaloo surrounding my erstwhile pupil George O'Dowd now transmogrified into a downmarket version of Danny La Rue", and concluded that George, far from being the "nonconformist divergent figure" suggested by the previous correspondent, had "simply climbed on the popular unisex bandwagon in order to make a bob or two". That was too much for George, who hit back in a letter which the publication ran

under the headline "GEORGE AND THE 'DRAGON'". Referring to Peter Dawson's previous remarks to the newspapers about his schooldays, George wrote: "Mr Peter Dawson may have been put out by my comment on television referring to him as a 'drag queen'. But he really should have taken into account the possibility that I might retaliate against his obnoxious press statements referring to my personal school history as 'a waste of time'. Mr Dawson made a fool of himself by joining in with the rest of the rabble. I was sure that at any moment, Mr Dawson would appear in a front-page picture exclusive in the *News of the World* holding the very cane he supposedly used to chastise me with. It had never occurred to me that my old headmaster could be so indignant and careless. We live and learn."

George concluded the attack on his headmaster with the suggestion – "If being head of the Professional Association of Teachers [*Peter Dawson's current position*] is not enough perhaps he could stand in some time for Mel Brooks".

All jolly japes, but once again is it a case of George using the media to put forward his own viewpoint? In that particular case it may have been justified, but George is one of the privileged few who can do it almost whenever he wants.

George even uses the media to carry out his personal and professional feuds in public. Not only have his disagreements with Marilyn been aired before millions, but his verbal scuffles with the notorious pop group, Frankie Goes To Hollywood, and Pete Burns of Dead Or Alive, have used up hundreds of inches of newsprint, doubtless helping to sell all their records.

And publicity can emanate from the most unlikely places. When the councillors of Thurles, the Tipperary birthplace of George's grandparents, rejected the suggestion that they should give the pop singer a civic welcome, George's father wrote an indignant – if lyrical – letter to the local

RED CARPET AND BOY GEORGE

The Crest,
171 Shooters Hill,
Woolwich,
London SE18 3HP.
29th April, 1984.

The Editor,
"Tipperary Star"

Dear Editor,
I write in response to a front page coverage, in the Sunday World, dated 18th April instant, titled, Irish Home Town Snubs Boy George, the article gave credit to Thurles town councillors as saying that if Boy George, "paid a visit to the town of Thurles, he would not merit the red carpet treatment, and a reference was implied that Boy George may give offence to the Bishop, who has his residence in Thurles".

When an Irish man goes home, he is made welcome by the smell of the turf fires, the mystery of the mountains, by the recognition of the very stones on the roads that he once trod, he meets the kinfolk and has the crack, he ponders at the place where loved ones rest, and he remembers.

The exiled does not expect, or indeed want, the red carpet treatment, for he sees the red carpet as the instrument that represents the imperial misfortune of his country and birthright.

While the town councillors of Thurles prepare for the impending visit by the President of the U.S.A. I may ask, what kind of new industry the town councillors are expecting the president to provide for the town of Thurles? Could it be that they are expecting devastating legacy, that in time, no one will be alive to remember?

George O'Dowd is the great grandson of the union in marriage of Martin Boyle and Katherine Cummings, late of the Old Pudding Lane; he has so many connections in the town of Thurles, living and dead, that perhaps the town councillors were rather unwise to publicly deride a now famous son of Ireland. Should my son every visit Thurles, it will only be to call in and say hello to the kinfolk, and perhaps, have a few old jars.

Yours sincerely,
JEREMIAH O'DOWD,
the Boyo's father.

newspaper, signing himself "the Boyo's father". Jerry O'Dowd was astonished at the reaction to his comments which were reprinted in newspapers right across Ireland. Not only did he discover several long-lost relatives but one of the councillors wrote back inviting George to do a concert in the town – providing yet another barrage of free publicity.

Even the up-market publications have acknowledged 'the Boy George Phenomenon' – something that would certainly not have happened had they not read about him in the popular press – with the society magazine, *The Tatler*, placing him second in its list of one hundred most famous people, ahead of both the Queen and Mrs Thatcher. Princess Diana came first, endorsing George's own opinion that she and he are the two most photographed English people in the world.

George knows he is very much a media person. He is highly visual and articulate, and quirky enough to intrigue a cross-section of the public most of whom would know nothing about him had they not seen him in the newspapers or on television. When George appeared on Terry Wogan's chat show he delighted millions of viewers who had previously regarded him as a freak. George loved that interview because the professional Wogan allowed him to take it over totally, gabbling away and laying down the law on almost any topic he chose. ". . .you talk a lot," said George to his host at one point. "Not tonight," cracked back Wogan. However, when Australia's top television chat show host asked George a question he did not like, he flew into a tantrum and threw his interviewer out of the room. And, although his flare-up may have made local headlines it is unlikely that George will be invited on to that particular show again.

George acknowledges that Fleet Street is powerful, but he is in the lucky position of being able to hit back. When Princess Margaret reportedly referred to him as an "over made-up tart" the story appeared in all the tabloids. George, full of righteous indignation, helped to keep the controversy running for several days, demanding a royal apology and insisting that he brings more money into the country than the Princess. One of the newspapers ran a poll among its readers who came up with a two-to-one result in support of George. But while George capitalised on the incident, Princess Margaret, as a member of the Royal Family, was not even able to answer back.

And, although George may damn the press for manipulating his image, it is, after all, something he has always done himself. In retrospect, he explains away his outburst at the Heathrow photographers as a deliberate ruse to change his image into something less like the Queen Mother which was not what he said at the time. And, however boring, boring, boring it is being photographed, without the cameras Boy George would not even have an image to change.

As he said himself recently in an indignant letter to the Daily Star ". . . let us not forget how important we are to each other . . ."

A chilly confrontation with Princess Margaret

17 The Last Word

Blonde, bearded and billowy . . .

*P*hilip Sallon was being bitchy. "George is on a sea-food diet at the moment. He sees food and he eats it! You know what they're calling him now? Boy *Gorge*, and it isn't short for gorgeous, either!"

Certainly, on holiday with Marilyn in Jamaica, George's weight had rocketted to around thirteen stone, but he still looked "really sweet" to the devoted fans waiting to greet him – blonde, bearded and billowy – when he arrived back at Heathrow. This time he and Marilyn were careful not to be photographed together at the airport, protecting themselves from another bout of suggestive publicity and another potential tiff. But, then, in this tight little circle of confidants, having spats is an occupational hazard.

Indeed, when Marilyn's first record got into the charts, Philip says George told him: "The only reason Marilyn mixes with you is because he's a failure." Philip was furious. "What fucking cheek! In other words, if you sell more records than someone else, they're not worth bothering with. Unbelievable. Let him go to hell, anyway!"

With his own recording contract securely wrapped up Philip had been too busy to join George and Marilyn in Jamaica and had therefore been lacking in sparring partners. However, he had plenty to do what with nurturing his voice for its EMI debut and running his club nights for the new generation of soft punks and cross-dressers. He had moved his Friday night Mud Club from Foubert's to the larger Busby's in Charing Cross Road and on the first night the clientele packed themselves on to the lazer-spliced dance floor to jerk to a mix of Motown and High Energy sounds spun by weird blonde disc-jockey Tasty Tim. Dress was optional, anything but "ordinary", so they came in dreadlocks and dark glasses, studs and sequins, braid and boas – almost identical to what the regulars once wore at a club called Louise's. One wild-haired blonde sported black plastic hot pants, pale blue tights and stiletto sandles on his size nine feet. Philip, very much the anxious host, had utilized his artistic talents of which his mother is so proud to decorate the club with enormous multi-coloured close-ups of male and female genitalia and the scrawled slogan *Make Love Not War.* Margo-'n'-Melanie, covered in florescent paint, spent the whole night dancing on barrels for which Philip paid them £10 each – money he might just as well have given directly to George since anything left over from their taxi fare home would certainly be spent on him.

George himself was doing a concert in Japan that night but, anyway, the London club scene no longer holds for him the magnetism it once did. He is now too famous to be able to escape the tourists and teenyboppers and insists: "I never wanted to be part of the Camden Palace scene and I don't now", referring to the music hall-turned-discotheque which Steve Strange re-gilded in Camden Town. Indeed, these days, George is a virtual recluse, venturing out at night only to visit close friends or dine at exclusive restaurants. On a rare and recent visit to Planets, George sat outside in the car with Philip for nearly three hours before Philip went into the club alone. Or George, with hatmaker Stephen Jones, might go to dinner to Steve Strange's north-west London flat where Steve – "I'm quite noted for my dinner parties" – will cook boeuf bourgignon or coq au vin while the three young men mull over what was, what is and what may yet be.

This is George O'Dowd's life today, simple, stylish and frequently solitary. Even

Philip – belle of the Mud Club ball

after concerts, while the rest of the band socialize in the bar, George will go straight to his room and usually to bed with a pile of his headed notepaper and a choice of flip one-liners to scrawl across the pages. No longer can he even go shopping himself apart from the occasional swift foray into small one-man shops like the cut-price linen one near Oxford Circus. Normally it is Bill Button, the Cockney ex-minicab driver who is George's personal assistant and faithful comrade, who buys him his make-up and postage stamps and anything else that he needs. He also drives George around in the brown Rover which replaced the white Mercedes – unless Marilyn is there to chauffeur him in his own convertible black VW Golf.

After leaving Goodge Street, George moved into Philip Sallon's tiny attic flat in Alma Square in smart St John's Wood which Philip's parents bought him years ago in the vain hope that their eccentric son would leave home. But Philip hated the flat – "a horrible little rabbit hutch. George didn't mind it but he wasn't stuck with it forever". Indeed, Philip intends to remain living with his parents, despite the constant antagonism – "I was born in this house and I'll never leave it".

George's former penthouse flat in St. John's Wood with flatmate Richard, *inset*

For George, however, the flat was ideal. He shared it with a friend of Philip's called Richard who worked on a fashion stall in the King's Road, finding it a relief to go home to someone totally uninvolved with the business of music. George lived there for about four years, eventually being forced reluctantly to leave by the dozens of Boy George clones camping on his doorstep. "Sundays started to become an event outside my house," admits George. "Hundreds of fans would turn up and it got to the point where it didn't matter if I was there or not – they'd all have a picnic and it was a sort of social occasion." One of his neighbours, Ann Bishop, a theatrical agent, remembers him looking no different from the other teenagers in the street when he went down to the newsagent or corner shop. "In those days he had short hair and he'd go out with no make-up and a pair of jeans looking just like everyone else," she recalls. So much so that one of the fans, failing to recognise him, asked him where Boy George lived. George obligingly pointed out his own flat to the girl. Ann Bishop used to see him and Marilyn and other friends leaving the flat to go to night clubs when she was walking her dog late at night. It was, however, a relief to his neighbours when, in 1983, he moved to an expensive service flat near Harrods, just one brown room, kitchen and bathroom, with his clothes piled all over the floor, living "a bit like a rat under paper".

But home, to George, is still where his parents live and he visits them often, especially for Sunday lunch. He gives them expensive presents to make their life more comfortable. "My own charity begins at home," he says. "I'm generous to my family although I'd never give my parents money. You take away people's dignity doing that." Says his mother, Dina: "George is not extravagant with money but he's extravagant with us." Just before *Do You Really Want To Hurt Me?* was released, George's father had a heart-attack. When he recovered consciousness he asked Dina not to tell George. "Obviously being as close as we are I knew it would upset him," says Jerry. When Dina did break the news to her son he went straight to the hospital with the first copy of his record to come off the presses. Now, closer to his father than he has ever been, he worries about him. "How's Dad," he asks his mother when he telephones. And if she replies "he's a bit down today", George suggests "does he want to go on holiday? Do *you* want to go, mum? I'll send you". Says his mother: "He wouldn't think nothing of it and it wouldn't matter what it cost. If I wanted to go I could go." So far, George has paid for his parents to go to the South of France, Spain and to his mother's home in Ireland. "He gives you things but he doesn't want to talk about it," says Dina. "When you're going 'ooh – that's lovely', he's going 'shut up, shut up now. Don't go on about it'. For Christmas he bought us a colour television for our bedroom and I thought it was a lovely present and he just went 'all right – don't go on about it'." According to his family, George is also shy when people pay him compliments. His brother Gerald recalls the time George took him and his girlfriend Tracy to see Billy Joel in concert. Realising who was in the audience the band suddenly broke into Culture Club's album hit *I'll Tumble 4 Ya* while George slid down his seat in embarrassment.

The family has two dogs – an alsation and a mongrel – and a huge ginger cat called Sparky. "George loves animals," says his mother loyally, but Gerald disagrees. And, in fact, George has always been rather nervous of dogs. Indeed, once at Terry's house, drinking coffee in the early hours of the morning, George vanished to go to the toilet and failed to return to his friends. After about twenty minutes Terry went to find out what had happened and discovered George hiding behind the toilet door afraid to come out because the family labrador was standing placidly outside. George made Terry hold the

"Mr Doughnut" and "Pig Face" at the Billy Joel concert to which George took his brother Gerald

dog before he dared to emerge.

It is a characteristic that Jerry doubtlessly understands better than anyone. Now their past differences have been healed, George confides in his father more than anyone else. They write each other affectionate notes and poems saying the things they are shy to discuss face to face. "When George doesn't want to say something to me direct he'll write me a note," says Jerry. "I understand him and he understands me. We can both of us tell if something is bothering the other one. I wrote one poem to him – a few verses about war – and he wrote back saying he'd keep it." Before he left for Japan, George visited his family on his birthday to collect his presents and share a couple of bottles of Champagne with them and then went back again the following day with a giant Father's Day card and gift for Jerry. The two men sat and chatted into the early hours of the morning and then as it was getting light Jerry drove George home to Knightsbridge in his battered old builder's van. "People can't believe their eyes when they see George in the van," says Gerald. "They think it can't be him. One night we took him home and three blokes in a Mini started shouting at him abusively, calling him a poofter, and George just leaned out the window and screamed 'bollocks' at them. He's never lost for an answer. Don't ever cut him up on the road or he'll give you a verbal volley."

For Gerald and his other brothers, George's fame can be an embarrassment. Richard, Kevin and Gerald have all had to put up with ribbing on their building sites about having a famous "poofter" for a brother. "Initially the family took quite a lot of stick because of George," admits Jerry. "They've all, thank God, learned to live with it. We're all very proud of George and he comes here and argues with his brothers and sister as if he was still a resident member of the household. There's no difference between them and they've all got this nice volatile relationship. They have a little shout at each other and disagree and stamp their individuality but they're all very proud of George."

Kevin and Richard, both builders, are married but Gerald, David and Siobhain still live with their parents. Gerald has given up working as a labourer and is training full-time to be an athlete; David is a writer and photographer on the local paper; and Siobhain has finished her A-levels. The boys bitterly resent suggestions that George gives them anything of his millions. "The first thing everyone asks me is 'how are you getting on now? George must be looking after you'," says Gerald. "It was a bit hard to start with but I don't mention him now. I've never actually got into a fight over him."

In the chintzy front room of their family

George and Gerald and their father outside the house in Shooters Hill

home, Gerald's boxing trophies share pride of place with George's gold and platignum discs which he has given to his mother. Here, at least, the superstar is treated like just another member of the family. Behind the upstairs toilet door there is a big poster of an ape busily working on a sewing machine. One of George's brothers has drawn a balloon coming out the monkey's mouth with the words: "I wish Boy George had a smaller bum!" Even today, George is sensitive about what he regards as his "big bum".

Most of the fans know where the O'Dowds live but they leave them more or less in peace. Letters often arrive addressed simply to "Boy George, Bexley Heath, England". Middle-aged women deliver birthday cards for George and even send the family St Patrick's Day cards. One evening, three skinheads were passing the house just as George was arriving home. Jerry was preparing for trouble when one of the skin-

Boxing trophies and gold discs in the O'Dowds' front room. Jerry with his three youngest sons – David, Gerald and George

heads spotted George and shouted out "hey, Boy George, great to see you!" When Culture Club first played at London's Lyceum, George booked a box for his entire family to see him. "There were hundreds and hundreds of kids all dressed like him," recalls Dina, "and I was going – 'oh, that's our Georgie up there'. I cried my eyes out – I couldn't believe it." Afterwards she reproached her son for not waving to her. "Mum, I was terrified," said George.

George often takes Philip or Marilyn or Jon home with him and they sit round the kitchen table and chat with his parents just as they do at Philip's home. And it is in these suburban family environments that George is happiest and most relaxed. These people – his family and close friends – are his mainstay. He needs the stability and continuity they provide to stay sane and successful in his increasingly pressured world. Yet, even in his parents' house, these days, he will often sit by himself in a corner and go through his fan mail. "It's funny, he loves the peace and quiet now," says his mother. At Christmas, George led the whole family in a sing-song, harmonizing *Old MacDonald Had A Farm*

while one of his relatives strummed on an old guitar.

George recalls the days when his parents would look at his outrageous appearance and tell him "you'll grow out of it someday. In ten years time you'll look back and think how stupid you looked."

"The truth," says George, "is the opposite. I seem to be going more over the top as I get older." Even so, off-stage and away from the cameras, he has become less flamboyant. He has discovered that when he dresses up, people assume he wants to be noticed whereas if he dresses casually they are more inclined to leave him alone.

And, although to the world, George is the ultimate in contemporary success, to his parents he is just another child to be put in his place if necessary. Dina still tells him off for swearing in front of ladies and does her best to warn him about the potential dangers of fame and fortune. "Always remember who you are and where you come from," she advises him. "That way you'll keep your feet on the ground." She admits "I'd hate him to end up as one of these rude, arrogant sort of people."

Her warnings are probably unnecessary for George is a strong enough character to withstand the pitfalls of success just as he has avoided the temptations. If he is rude and arrogant on occasions then it is because that is what he has always been. In his headmaster's words, George has always been consistent and that is true of every aspect of his life. He is still as likely to use the "Ladies" as the "Gents" if he feels like it, is still unpunctual, greedy – "my table manners *are* different from other people's" – and mischievous. One friend recounts how whenever he has specifically asked him not to repeat a bit of gossip to the person involved George has gone out of his way to do just that. By the same token, George will always chat to old friends if he bumps into them. "Don't be too shy to say 'hello' just because I'm famous now," he recently told

Still as likely to use the "Ladies" as the "Gents"

Simple, stylish and frequently solitary . . .

one of the girls he knew at the time of Louise's. And, at the height of his popularity, he went skinny-dipping in Regents Park lake with a few friends from his squatting days – "just for old times' sake".

Unlike Marilyn who has, according to old friends, become more starlike over the last few months, George is unchanged, with the same strengths and weaknesses he possessed even as a child. The only difference is that now his energy and dedication have a purposeful and profitable direction.

And while some of his former friends insist that they always knew George would be something special, others confess that his success has come as a complete surprise to them. Jane is typical of the latter. "When I got married and found my own happiness I thought 'God, how is George going to end up?'" she admits. "I often thought of him as an old man – gay, dressing up, living in a squat with no money and no comforts and I felt sad for him."

As ever, it is George who is having the last word.

Photo Credits

Snowdon/Camera Press
Derek Ridgers/Ace/Sunday Times
Iain McKell
Justine Thomas/Ace
Brian Moody/Colorific/Sunday Magazine
Terence Spencer/Camera Press
Graham Smith
Graham Wiltshire/Camera Press
Neil Matthews
Nicola Tyson
Lorrie Graham
Richard Young/Rex Features
Elizabeth-Ann Colville
Andria Law
Melanie Amerasekera
Margo Bovell

Associated Press
Camera Press
London Express News and Features
London Features International
Pictorial Press
Press Association
Raymond's of Derby
Syndication International
Newsweek cover courtesy of Newsweek
Cartoons courtesy of The Sun/News of the World